Copyright © 2018 Angela B. Pan Photography
All rights reserved

ISBN-10: 1975605535
ISBN-13: 978-1975605537

No part of this book may be reproduced, stored in a retrieval system, or transmitted, in any form or by any means, electronic, mechanical, photocopying, microfilming, recording, or otherwise, without written permission from the publisher.

Printed in the United States of America.

DEDICATED TO NAI NAI PAN

TABLE *of* CONTENTS

INTRODUCTION *1*

LINCOLN MEMORIAL *5*

WAR MEMORIALS *27*

WASHINGTON MONUMENT *49*

TIDAL BASIN *63*

MEMORIAL GARDENS *107*

GOVERNMENT BUILDINGS *119*

OUTSIDE THE MALL *147*

CONCLUSION *201*

ACKNOWLEDGMENTS *202*

ABOUT *203*

INTRODUCTION

My parents moved to the Washington, D.C., metro area soon after they graduated from college in Taiwan. At a young age I remember asking my dad why they chose to settle in this area. I mean, they could have lived anywhere in the United States. Plus, there are like no beaches around here! Yet somehow my entire family, even extended family, has made their home here at some point in their lives.

So, why Washington? Dad answered my question. With pride in his eyes and his fist in the air, his lips clenched, and his nostrils flaring so hard I wondered if he was still breathing, he said:

"Because it's the capital!" That was all I needed to hear.

If you ask any of us who live here, we will say that living in this city is more than just about politics and government. It's a lifestyle. It's a feeling. It's an honor.

Some of my best memories growing up in Virginia took place when my family or school class would visit Washington, D.C. It was only twenty minutes away from our home, but I still remember going on elementary school field trips to the Smithsonian Museum and being really excited about the rocks and gems in the National Museum of Natural History. Visiting the city with my parents at five years old, my mom posed me for pictures in front of the cherry blossoms and other beautiful flowers. And I never said no to ice cream from the food trucks lining the streets of the National Mall. But my favorite part was always just walking around the Mall, exploring.

The experience only improved when I held a camera in my hand. See, I fell in love with photography when I was in high school. Once I took that very first photo class, I was addicted. I knew I had found my passion in life. Whenever I had school assignments, or just free time in general, I'd find myself wandering through D.C. with my camera, making pictures.

And I haven't stopped since. I've spent years walking around the capital city, observing and capturing its beauty in photographs. I love checking out new places and revisiting the old, familiar ones. Sometimes I'll even find myself purposely walking the long way to some places, just to see things from a new perspective. I find it truly exciting and fulfilling to display the city in different kinds of light and at different angles. I have also learned to appreciate the little things...like watching the evening light hit the Washington Monument as daylight slowly fades to night or watching the little ducklings grow from spring to the end of summer. Sometimes I find it hard to explain why I love photography so much, but it is the creative medium I use to share how I see the world with others--as a place of amazing color, line, shape, beauty, and peace.

So, I want to share my experiences with you to enhance your experience of my favorite city. This book isn't filled with facts, statistics, or the history of Washington. It's about appreciating its beauty...capturing its essence in your heart! I hope you will use my images, camera settings, and experience as inspirations to create your own.

I challenge you to really think about what it's like for you to be in Washington, D.C. and then bring all those emotions and stories to your images. Experiment, and shoot what makes you feel happy. Show me your own story of our nation's capital, and I'll show you mine.

This book will help get you started. But believe me, there is so much more in this city just waiting to be explored. You're gonna love it!

Here's a fun game to play on your journey through this photo collection. It's kind of my own little version of Where's Waldo? Here's how it goes: The Washington Monument is D.C.'s tallest structure. You can pretty much see it anywhere in the city if you look around. So, as a side search while you explore my photographs, count how many times you see it in this book. The answer will be given at the very end.

By the way, there are some museums, memorials, and monuments I was not able to include here due to image copyright rules. I've included information on these particular places as recommendations for your discovery, without including their images. Maybe you will create your own!

Angela Pan, 2018

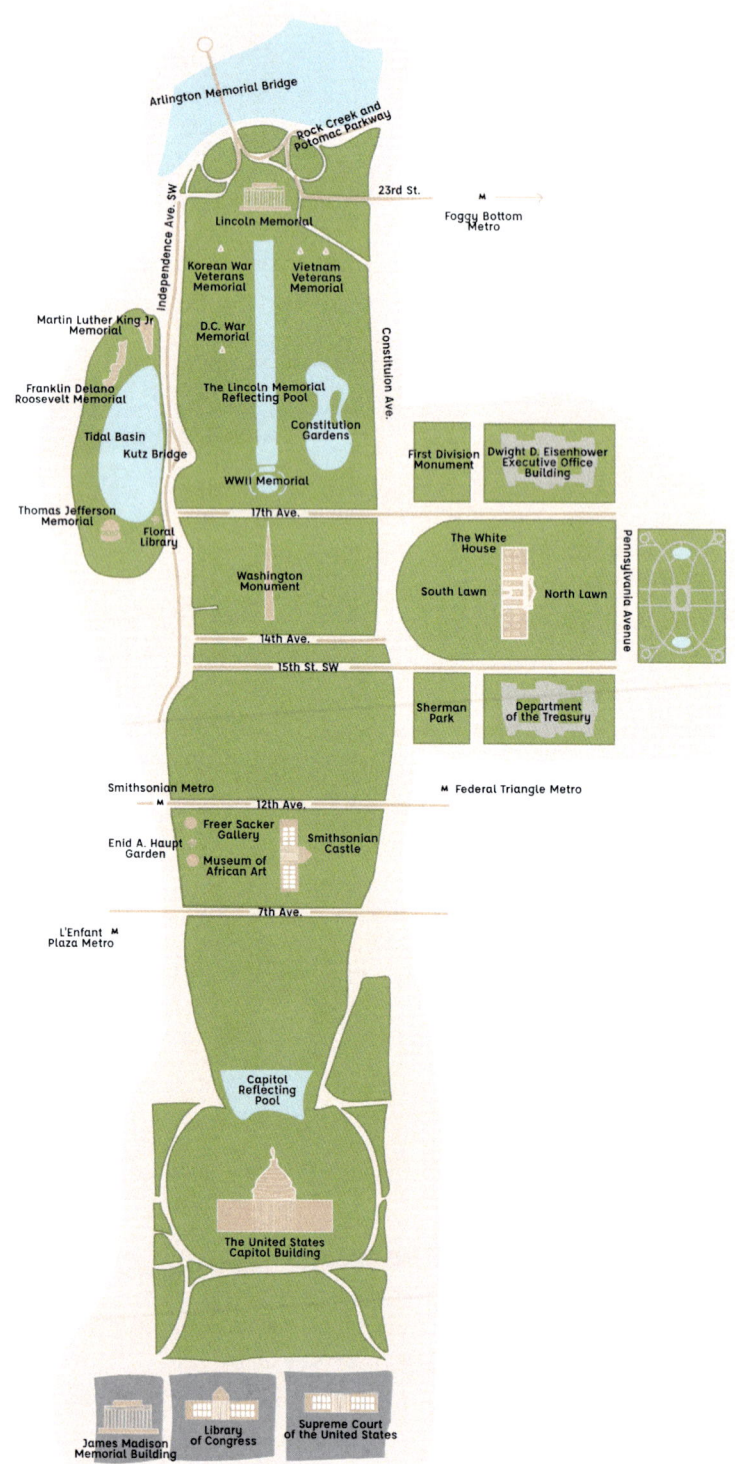

ANGELA B. PAN — THE NATIONAL MALL

THE NATIONAL MALL

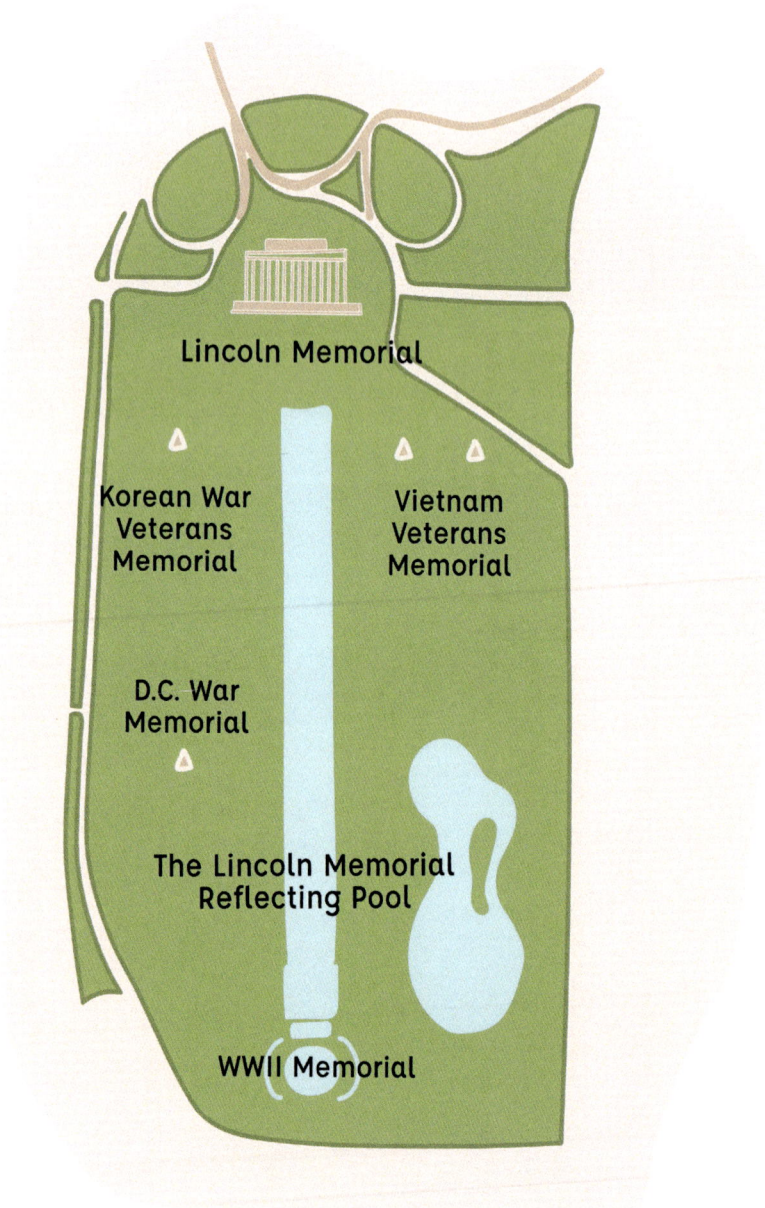

LINCOLN MEMORIAL
and
LINCOLN REFLECTING POOL

LINCOLN MEMORIAL

The Lincoln Memorial is one of my favorite sites on the National Mall. It's the first thing I see when I drive into the city from Virginia, and it makes me super happy. I dunno; it sort of feels like home. I love how, at any given moment of the day, you'll see people just hanging out on the steps of this Memorial. There's no better place to sit and soak in the beauty of the nation's capital, or to just stand amidst so much rich history. If you look closely enough, you can see the exact spot where Martin Luther King, Jr. stood to deliver his "I Have a Dream" speech in 1963. It's engraved into the marble steps. If that doesn't give you chills, then I don't know what would! And, if you squint your eyes enough, you can actually see Jenny drudging across the reflecting pool screaming at Forrest in the movie, Forrest Gump. Just kidding about that last one, but it'd be pretty cool if you could. "Forrrrrest!"

In all seriousness, the Lincoln Memorial is stunning. The best part is that you can walk all around the base of the Memorial for 360-degree views of this baby! It's the perfect spot for sunrise or sunset photography.

However I'm more partial to the early morning. It's the only time of day you can photograph the Memorial without risking the possibility of hundreds of people in your shot.

You can also climb the steps and walk all around the Memorial for an elevated view of surrounding areas. You'll find the Vietnam Veterans Memorial to the left, the Korean War Veterans Memorial to the right, the Lincoln Memorial Reflecting Pool in front, and the World War II Memorial just beyond that. It's the perfect place to start your photo adventure.

1/2 sec F/5.6 ISO 400
Sony A7II 16-35mm
Try to pay attention to the details that fascinate you. For this image, I was really trying to study the relationship of the Lincoln statue to the powerful words behind him.

1.6 seconds F/7.1 ISO 400
Sony A7II 16-35mm
The best part about these memorials is that they are open twenty-four hours and there are always U.S. Park police around to keep you safe. This was taken around 1:00 a.m. I didn't wake up at this time. I was on a photowalk called "Midnight at the Monuments" with the Instagram group @walkwithlocals. It was awesome to see what the memorials looked like in the middle of the night.

1/2 sec F/6.3 ISO 250
Sony A7II 16-35mm
As I set up my shot on the south side of the Memorial, the early morning light made the structure glow pink and created new leading lines in the architecture that usually aren't seen. Again, visiting the Memorial in the early morning hours will be your best chance at getting images without people in them.

1/4 sec F/5.0 ISO 320
Sony A7II 16-35mm

As you're entering the Memorial, look at the lines created by the columns. They make for a great framing or line to your main subject.

3.2 seconds F/9 ISO 100
Canon 5D Mark II 24-105mm
Don't let the rain ruin your trip. Take shelter and wait for it to pass. Then use the opportunity to find some cool reflections in the water. And, most of the time after rain, the sky will be glowing.

1 second F/4 ISO 640
Canon 5D Mark II 24-105mm

While it was snowing the door to the museum was open, which allowed for a unique view of President Lincoln. Placing his face in the center towards the right was a play on the "Rule of Thirds" photographic composition rule.

ANGELA B. PAN   LINCOLN MEMORIAL

2.5 seconds F/8 ISO 640
Sony A7II 28-70mm

After a rainstorm, many gorgeous puddles can be found around the Lincoln Memorial. Just look down and don't worry about other people thinking you're crazy for shooting the ground! Tripods will work, but sometimes you will need to get even closer. Don't be afraid to place your camera on the ground, either.

2.5 seconds F/6.3 ISO 320
Sony A7II 16-35mm

Taken on the Rock Creek and Potomac Parkway, right behind the Lincoln Memorial. For this image, I had two tripod legs in the puddle and one on the sidewalk. My main focus was to get the reflection in the puddle, but also to use the leading lines from the car trails to bring the viewer into the image. Be patient, and find the elements that will help your viewer "read" the image.

ANGELA B. PAN   LINCOLN MEMORIAL

**1/1000 sec F/4.0 ISO 100
Canon 5D Mark II 24-105mm**
This bird's-eye view of the National Mall is a unique perspective that can only be seen from the top of the Washington Monument.

ANGELA B. PAN   LINCOLN MEMORIAL

1/3200 sec F4 ISO 400
Sony A7II 28-70mm

After it rained I was walking across the street to my parked car. I noticed the reflection in the puddle. Luckily, there were no cars coming, so I was able to grab this shot from the middle of the street.

LINCOLN MEMORIAL

FAVORITE TIME OF DAY TO SHOOT:
Sunrise

CLOSEST METRO:
Foggy Bottom

ADDRESS:
2 Lincoln Memorial Circle NW, Washington, DC 20037

SUGGESTED PARKING:
Constitution Ave, Rock Creek and Potomac Parkway NW, 22nd St NW
Pay attention to the street signs. Some of it is permit-only parking.

FOR MORE INFO:
http://www.abpan.com/book/lincolnmemorial

the LINCOLN MEMORIAL REFLECTING POOL

In between the Lincoln Memorial and the World War II Memorial, is the reflecting pool.

It is my go-to place when I don't know what to shoot, because no matter what, you can get some seriously killer shots here.

Depending on the time of day, it's best to stand in front of the Lincoln at sunrise and behind the WWII memorial at sunset. These are best practices, but every rule is meant to be broken! Try it out, and if you don't like it, it's just a fifteen-minute walk to the other end.

I recommend just sitting down at the edge of the pool and taking time with your shots. Get down low and just enjoy the scenery. It's a great place to slow down and people watch, too.

1/40 sec F14 ISO 250
Sony A7II 28-70mm
Sitting right at the edge of the reflecting pool in front of the Lincoln Memorial, enjoying the early morning sky, yielded this glorious image.

(image on page 21-22)
15 seconds F11 ISO 400
Sony A7II 16-35mm
This photo was taken about twenty minutes before sunset. The sun was out, but it wasn't bright. I noticed how fast the clouds were moving, so I used my neutral density filter to slow the shutter speed and capture this movement. The contrast of the moving clouds against the fixed trees and Lincoln Memorial make this image much more interesting. Also, a longer exposure will blur out anybody who may be walking along the side of the reflecting pool in your frame.

1/80 sec F/5.6 ISO 100
Sony A7II 28-70mm
These walkways along the side of the reflecting pool are beautiful at any time of the year. This was taken right after a snowfall. I love how the trees at the end form a heart. Every other season, these trees make for a great canopy. Check out the leading lines, repetition, and patterns that this area can create...and have fun!

1/80 sec F/5.6 ISO 200
Sony A7II 16-35mm

Get down low and capture the reflection in the water. Just don't put your tripod in the water. I've seen many people do this. It's not good for the reflecting pool or the ducks!

8 seconds F/5.6 ISO 200
Sony A7II 16-35mm
The Washington Monument glows here from the setting sun's light.

ANGELA B. PAN — REFLECTING POOL

1/12 sec F/7.1 ISO 200
Canon 5D Mark II 17-40mm
A PANoramic view from the side of the Reflecting Pool. I stitched together 5 different exposures into one image using photoshop.

THE LINCOLN MEMORIAL REFLECTING POOL

FAVORITE TIME OF DAY TO SHOOT
Sunrise

CLOSEST METRO:
Foggy Bottom

ADDRESS:
2 Lincoln Memorial Circle NW, Washington, DC 20037

SUGGESTED PARKING:
Constitution Ave, Rock Creek and Potomac Parkway NW, 22nd St NW

FOR MORE INFO:
http://www.abpan.com/book/reflectingpool

AMERICAN WAR MEMORIALS

AMERICAN WAR MEMORIALS

It's really hard to generalize thoughts about these war memorials. There is no way to describe them, other than emotional. Every time I walk through them, I like to take a moment to express my gratitude to those who have served our country. I don't know the whole story of what these men and women had to go through to give me the life I have, but I'm so grateful for it. It's memorials like these that show our appreciation to them.

Other suggested War Memorials to photograph:
Korean War Memorial and Navy-Merchant Marine Memorial

VIETNAM VETERANS MEMORIAL

Located to the north of the Lincoln Memorial, the Vietnam Veterans Memorial is probably the most well-known of the war memorials on the National Mall. Oftentimes, I'll run my fingers over the names of the soldiers and say, "Thanks." Sometimes you'll see people placing pieces of paper and lead pencil on the stone Memorial, rubbing names onto them as a keepsake of loved-ones. Other times, you'll see flowers lining the wall. All these interactions with the wall could help tell your story of what it was like for you to visit.

> *My favorite part of the Vietnam Veterans Memorial is all the reflections it generates. You can get some great ones from here of the Washington Monument, Lincoln Memorial, and even of other visitors if you take the time to look for them.*

ANGELA B. PAN — VIETNAM VETERANS

ANGELA B. PAN — 32 — VIETNAM VETERANS

(photo on pages 31-32)
1 second F/5.6 ISO 100
Canon 5D Mark II 17-40mm

Pay attention to the wall; it is so reflective and shiny. You can capture some great reflections here. This was taken during an especially colorful sunrise. I was the only one at the Memorial, so I was able to take full advantage of the wall. Just make sure you're not in the shot yourself if you don't want to be!

1 second F/5.6 ISO 100
Canon 5D Mark II 17-40mm

Looking east at sunrise. My intention was to use the leading lines from the wall, the walk area, and chain fencing to lead the viewer's eye to the gorgeous sunrise and Washington Monument. The reflections of the trees in the wall were just an added bonus that help frame the Monument. Having everything centered and lined up was key for this image.

ANGELA B. PAN — VIETNAM VETERANS

1/4 sec F/5.6 ISO 400
Sony A7II 28-70mm
Many times you will find gifts, like this flower, left for the veterans. Try including them in your image to tell your story.

VIETNAM VETERANS MEMORIAL

FAVORITE TIME OF DAY TO SHOOT:
Sunrise

CLOSEST METRO:
Foggy Bottom

ADDRESS:
5 Henry Bacon Dr NW, Washington, DC 20245

SUGGESTED PARKING:
Constitution Ave, Rock Creek and Potomac Parkway NW, 22nd St NW

FOR MORE INFO:
http://www.abpan.com/book/vietnamveterans

NATIONAL WORLD WAR II MEMORIAL

This memorial is beautiful, but very big. It can be difficult to shoot in its entirety because it's so wide. If you want to capture the whole thing, I recommend shooting with your wide-angle lens. If you don't have one, then I suggest walking across 17th St. NW, closer to the Washington Monument, and shooting from there. That's the only way you'll be able to contain everything.

Otherwise, there are little details in this Memorial that make you want to walk the whole thing. First, each pillar represents a different state or U.S. territory. It's fun to locate all the places you have been or your home state. Secondly, the water feature in the middle is obviously the main attraction, but you'll also see little waterfalls in the back of this Memorial that create great reflections of the Lincoln Memorial from far away. And, last but not least, there is a panel of stars you have to see! Each one represents one hundred people who gave their lives in World War II. It's remarkable how many of them are there…4,048 stars.

1 second F/3.5 ISO 200
Sony A7II 28-70mm
With all the city lights, it's difficult to capture the stars in Washington. Taken from across 17th St. NW, this vantage point allowed me to capture most of the memorial in one frame.

1/50 sec F/5.6 ISO 100
Canon 5D Mark II 17-40mm
Four images stitched together to create a whole PANoramic image in Photoshop. To get the best panoramic images, I recommend shooting them vertically with your camera. You'll get much more in the frame than you would if you shot them horizontally.

ANGELA B. PAN　　　　　　　　　　38　　　　　　　　　　WWII MEMORIAL

15 seconds F/5 ISO 500
Sony A7II 16-35mm
A lot of times you will want to look west to watch a beautiful sunset. This particular evening was cloudy and there were great colors all around. Don't forget to look behind you! This was a sunset view, facing east.

1 second F/4.5 ISO 320
Sony A7II 16-35mm
Reflections can be found anywhere. Just be on the lookout!

8.0 seconds F/5.6 ISO 200
Sony A7II 28-70mm
Taken at 12:30 a.m. with @walkwithlocals. The water fountains are turned off, but the lights are still glowing. I took full advantage of the still water to capture the Memorial's reflection.

1/6 sec F/22 ISO 50
Sony A7II 16-35mm
A great way to spend a morning is to sit at the edge of the water and watch the sunrise. This was a handheld shot, but I made a conscious effort to make sure the water flow in the foreground did not block the water on the other side. Little details like that can really make or break an image.

NATIONAL WORLD WAR II MEMORIAL

FAVORITE TIME OF DAY TO SHOOT:
Sunrise

CLOSEST METRO:
Federal Triangle

ADDRESS:
1750 Independence Ave. SW, Washington, DC 20024

SUGGESTED PARKING:
Constitution Ave, Tidal Basin Paddle Boats parking lot

FOR MORE INFO:
http://www.abpan.com/book/wwiimemorial

DISTRICT *of* COLUMBIA
WAR MEMORIAL

This Memorial commemorates local residents who served in World War I. It isn't the biggest memorial, and it's kind of off to the side, all on its own, but it is beautiful. My favorite part is its symmetry. From the columns to the trees that surround the area, and the placement of the landscaping, it is one of those places where it's easy to get a great picture. The key here is simplicity. For some reason, not a lot of people ever visit or even know it's here. It can be a great spot to find some quiet time in an area that's busy with people twenty-four hours a day.

1/80 sec F/5.6 ISO 100
Sony A7II 16-35mm

Taken the morning of a snow storm. This memorial is unique because it's one of the few circular ones in the District. The snow is a perfect blanket to simplify this image down to the repeating lines.

**1.3 seconds F/13 ISO 200
Sony A7II 28-70mm**

The D.C. War Memorial is usually very quiet. So, you can visit it in the middle of the day, or at sunset, and still not have people in your image. It's also a great place to bring a friend for portrait work.

ANGELA B. PAN — DC WAR MEMORIAL

ANGELA B. PAN — DC WAR MEMORIAL

DISTRICT OF COLUMBIA WAR MEMORIAL

FAVORITE TIME OF DAY TO SHOOT:
Sunrise

CLOSEST METRO:
Foggy Bottom

ADDRESS:
1964 Independence Ave SW, Washington, DC 20227

SUGGESTED PARKING:
Ohio Dr

FOR MORE INFO:
http://www.abpan.com/book/dcwarmemorial

1/2 sec F/5.0 ISO 400
Canon 5D Mark II 70-200mm
The pink moon rises over the D.C. War Memorial viewed from the reflecting pool. It may be hard to spot during the day, but the glowing lights from the Memorial made it easy to spot at night.

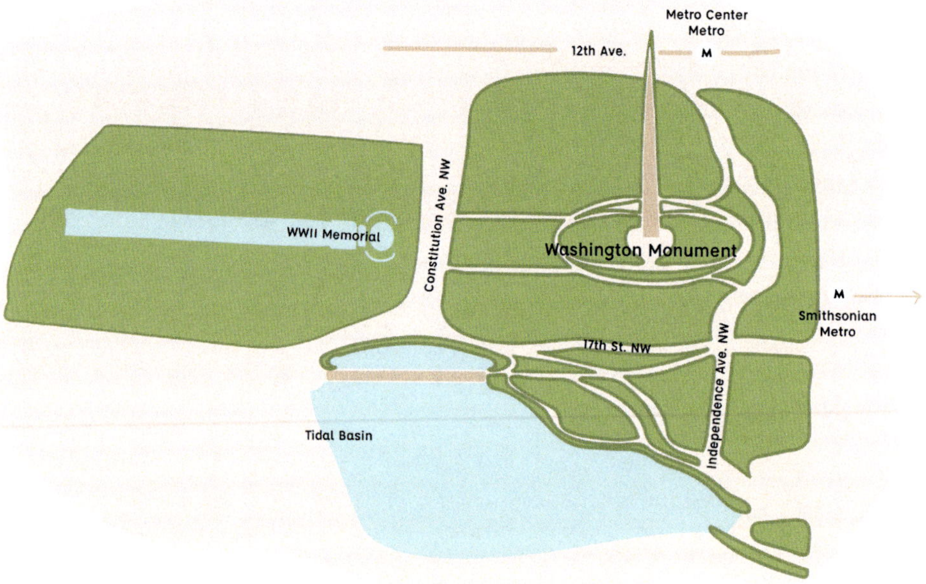
Metro Center
Metro
12th Ave.
M
Constitution Ave. NW
WWII Memorial
Washington Monument
M
Smithsonian
Metro
17th St. NW
Independence Ave. NW
Tidal Basin

WASHINGTON MONUMENT

WASHINGTON MONUMENT

The centerpiece of the city -- the Washington Monument. Every time I see it, I get a feeling of happiness. To me, it it symbolizes everything that I love about the city. Walk around it, walk right up to it and try different angles. It's a great place to catch sunrise or sunset. If you pay attention, you will see some great framing possibilities, a lot of leading lines, and it even change colors when the sun hits it at the right time. I think some people can find it difficult or intimidating to capture the Washington Monument because of its height. It's so iconic, but don't worry, you don't have to capture the entire thing to tell your story.

1/80 sec F/6.3 ISO 250
Sony A7II 16-35mm

Walking from the Tidal Basin to the Washington Monument, I saw a clearing of trees and thought it would be great for framing. The light on the Monument helps make this image stand out powerfully.

ANGELA B. PAN   WASHINGTON MONUMENT

(photo on pages 55-56)
1/10 sec F/7.1 ISO 200
Sony A7II 16-35mm

For this image, I used the walkway as a leading line to the Washington Monument and the fantastic light that was being cast on to it at sunset.

ANGELA B. PAN   WASHINGTON MONUMENT

1/4 sec F/5.6 ISO 100
Canon 5D Mark II 17-40mm

Shot from the base of the Washington Monument as a storm was approaching. I used the monument itself to divide the colorful sky and used the flags, pavment, and seating benches to draw the viewer into the image, a PANoramic shot of twenty images combined. This is an example of how you don't have to shoot the whole Washington Monument to capture its essence. My favorite part of this image is the transition from warm tones to cool tones.

ANGELA B. PAN　　　　　　　WASHINGTON MONUMENT

ANGELA B. PAN   55   WASHINGTON MONUMENT

ANGELA B. PAN — WASHINGTON MONUMENT

1/2 sec F/6.3 ISO 320
Sony A7II 16-35mm
These benches can be great for leading lines. The flags can make for great framing, as well. I love how none of them look exactly the same.

1/20 sec F/5.6 ISO 250
Canon 5D Mark II 24-105mm
There's this great tree right next to the Monument. I captured it after a light dusting of snow. I love this photo in black and white because it looks like it could have been taken anywhere, at any time of day. But nope, it's right next to the Washington Monument.

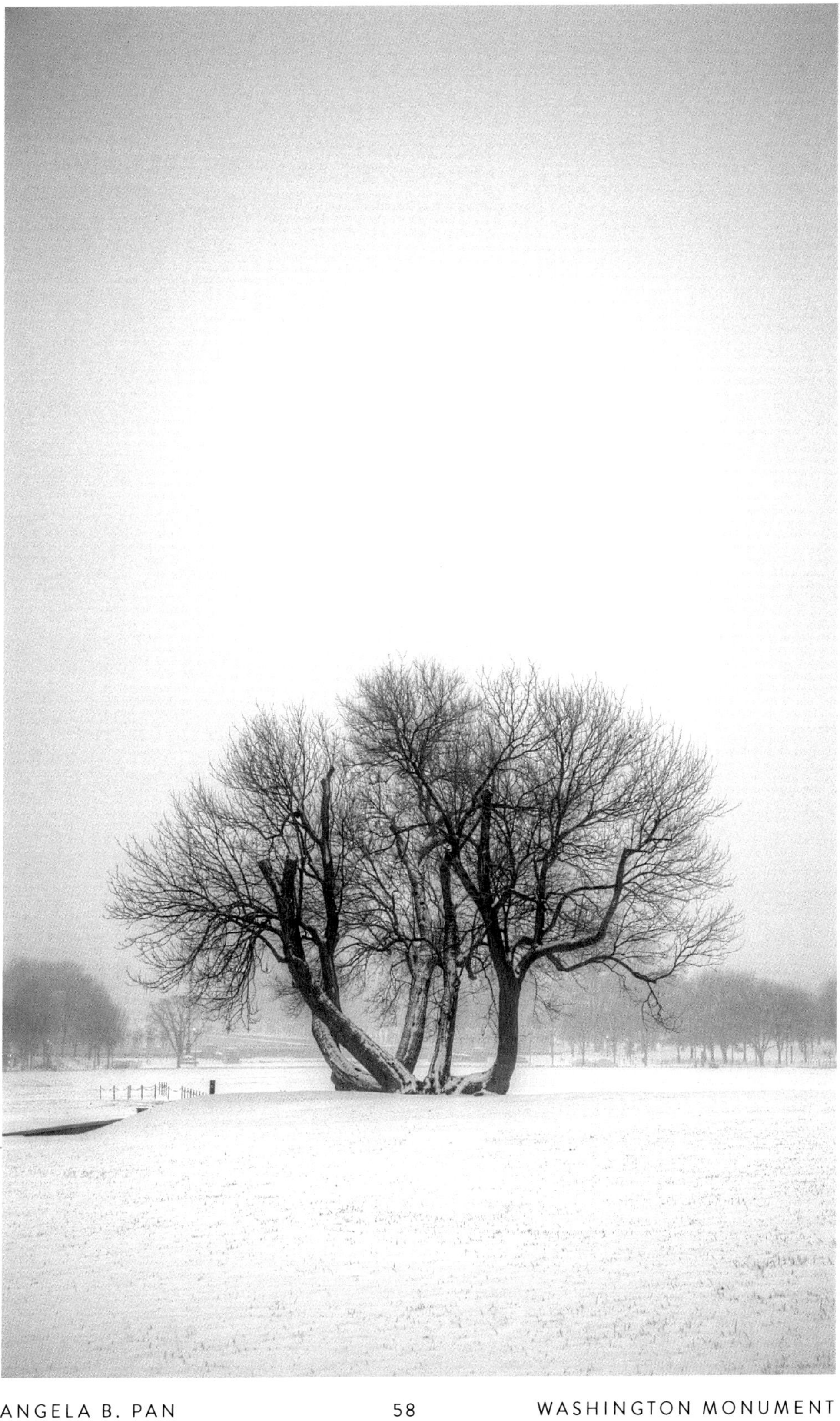

ANGELA B. PAN — WASHINGTON MONUMENT

ANGELA B. PAN 60 WASHINGTON MONUMENT

(photo on pages 59-60)
1/30 sec F/8 ISO 160
Sony A7II 28-70mm

Most of my images have no people in them; however, adding people can really help tell your story. Singling them out can make the image easier to read and less chaotic. It can be difficult, though. Try picking out one or two individuals from a crowd. This can add interest and emotion, or it can accentuate scale. It may take a while, but the moment you capture can be well worth it!

1/25 sec F/5.6 ISO 250
Sony A7II 16-35mm

From the bottom of a tiny hill, I bent down enough to line up the base of the trees with the base of the monument, hiding everything in between. It was this slight camera position adjustment that made a light coating of snow look like it was so much more.

WASHINGTON MONUMENT

FAVORITE TIME OF DAY TO SHOOT:
Sunset

CLOSEST METRO:
Smithsonian, Farragut West or McPherson Square

ADDRESS:
2 15th St NW, Washington, DC 20024

SUGGESTED PARKING:
Constitution Ave, Jefferson Dr SW, Madison Dr NW

FOR MORE INFO:
http://www.abpan.com/book/monument

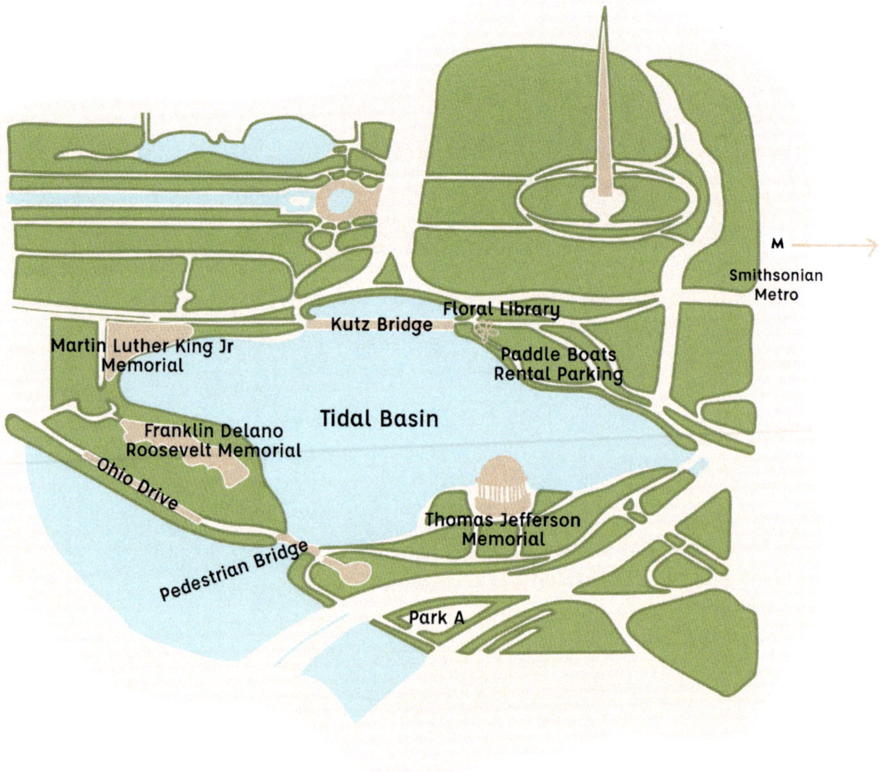
M
Smithsonian
Metro
Floral Library
Kutz Bridge
Martin Luther King Jr
Memorial
Paddle Boats
Rental Parking
Tidal Basin
Franklin Delano
Roosevelt Memorial
Ohio Drive
Thomas Jefferson
Memorial
Pedestrian Bridge
Park A

TIDAL BASIN

TIDAL BASIN

The Tidal Basin is a little off to the side of the National Mall, which usually means it is less crowded than other areas, and it's one of my favorite places to shoot. On a calm day, you can get amazing reflections in the water. After a rain shower, the marble of the Jefferson Memorial is so shiny and looks so new, you almost don't want to walk on it.

There is so much to see at the Franklin Delano Roosevelt Memorial. It's divided into several sections along the southwest part of the Tidal Basin. My favorite part are the water features. It makes a great background for portraits.

And the newest edition to the memorials, the Martin Luther King, Jr. Memorial, is a place to just stand and soak in all the beautiful views around it. You could spend a whole afternoon walking the Tidal Basin and not get bored. As you walk about, you'll notice views of the Washington Monument and the U.S. Capitol. It's so cool to see…and photograph!

(photo on pages 67-68)
2.0 seconds F/5.6 ISO 250
Sony A7II 28-70mm

I try to arrive at my location ready to shoot at least thirty minutes prior to sunrise.

Sometimes that will be the only time you will see color in the sky. This was taken on the pedestrian bridge right before all the color went away. (See map for exact position.)

the JEFFERSON MEMORIAL

My favorite feature of the Jefferson Memorial is its circular shape. The only other building like it is the D.C. War Memorial, which makes the Jefferson super-easy to identify when looking at pictures. Entering the Memorial, you get a feeling of happiness because the column openings allow so much sunlight in that it makes the memorial even more welcoming and fun to walk through. President Jefferson's statute itself is gigantic. And he's the only U.S. President represented in the memorials in a standing position.

3.2 seconds F/9 ISO 125
Sony A7II 16-35mm
Taken from behind the Jefferson Memorial, it's very interesting to see this building from different angles. My favorite part about most of the memorials and monuments is that you can walk all around them for 360-degrees of potential photo-goodness!

ANGELA B. PAN — JEFFERSON MEMORIAL

ANGELA B. PAN — JEFFERSON MEMORIAL

10 seconds F/5.6 ISO 1000
Sony A7II 16-35mm
Taken along the side of the Jefferson Memorial. The steps make for great leading lines and reflections, especially after a rainstorm has just passed.

1/200 sec F/7.1 ISO 160
Sony A7II 16-35 mm

Across from the Jefferson, taken at the Paddle Boats parking lot. It was a conscious decision to point my camera up a little bit to incorporate the tree branch. The darkness from above really makes your eye go straight to the main subject, which is the row of swans.

(photo on pages 73-74)
2.5 seconds F/5.6 ISO 125
Canon 5D Mark II 17-40mm
Early morning light shining through the columns around President Thomas Jefferson. Pay attention to framing and balance in your composition.

2.5 seconds F/5.6 ISO 125
Canon 5D Mark II 17-40mm
Through the columns of the memorial; I purposely got low to make the Jefferson figure look even bigger.

**1/160 sec F/7.1 ISO 200
Sony A7II 16-35mm**
At sunrise, standing in the Paddle Boats parking lot. When the water is calm, you can get some great reflections at Tidal Basin.

ANGELA B. PAN 73 JEFFERSON MEMORIAL

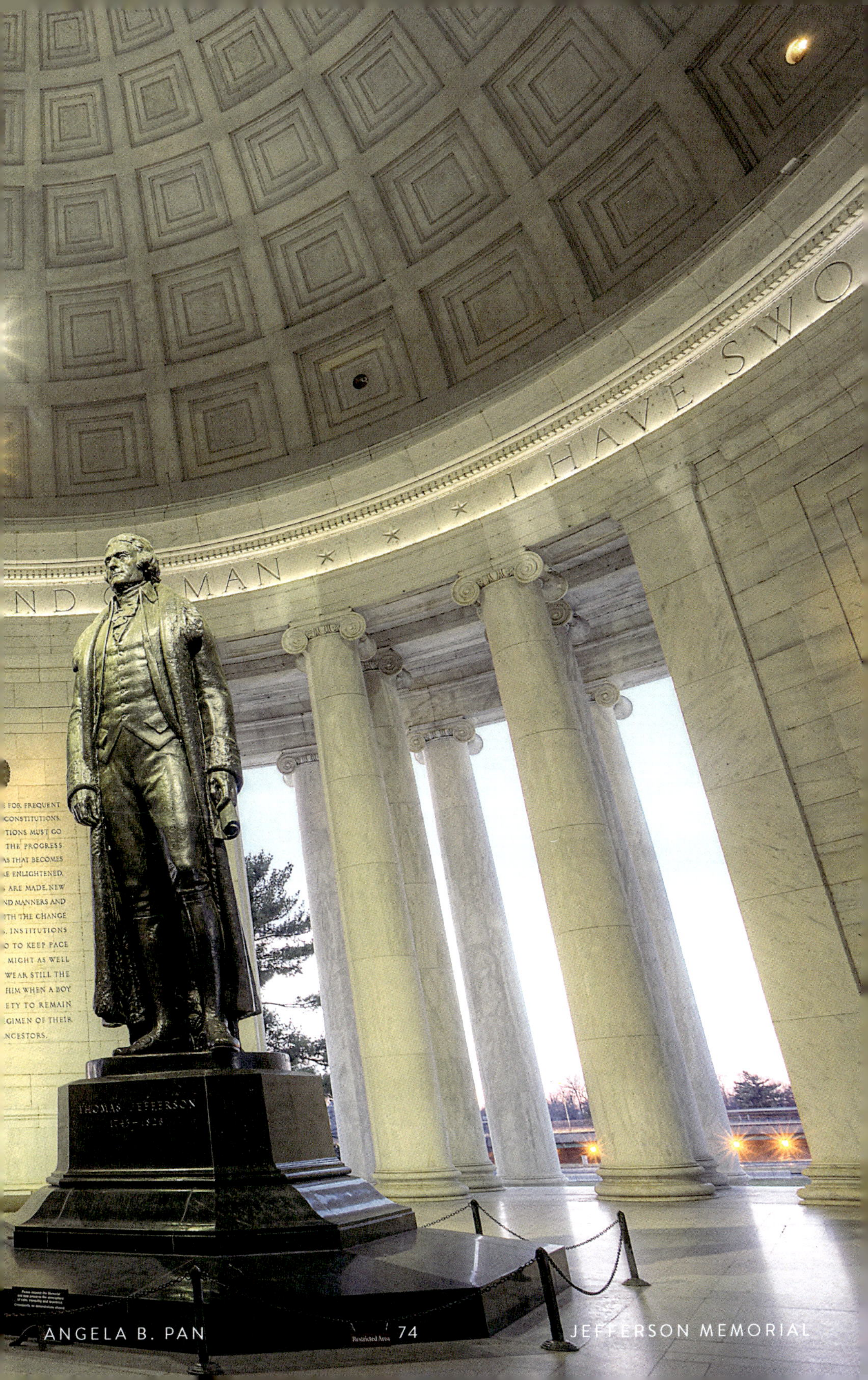
I HAVE SWO
MAN
THOMAS JEFFERSON
1743–1826
Restricted Area

**1/20 sec F/6.3 ISO 200
Sony A7II 16-35mm**

Taken from the footbridge, sitting in the middle of the sidewalk, I was able to capture this unique frame. It was taken at sunrise, so I wasn't in anyone's way setting it up. Try taking this with a wide-angle lens.

THE JEFFERSON MEMORIAL

FAVORITE TIME OF DAY TO SHOOT:
Sunset

CLOSEST METRO:
Smithsonian

ADDRESS:
701 E Basin Dr SW, Washington, DC 20242

SUGGESTED PARKING:
Ohio Dr, Park A

FOR MORE INFO:
http://www.abpan.com/book/jefferson

the **FLORAL LIBRARY**

In its own little corner of the Tidal Basin, the Floral Library is a quick and easy must-see. There's always something beautiful blooming in the spring, summer, and fall seasons. Sorry, winter!

1/50 sec F/7.1 ISO 100
Sony A7II 28-70mm
Shot in April, when the Floral Library is at its most vibrant!

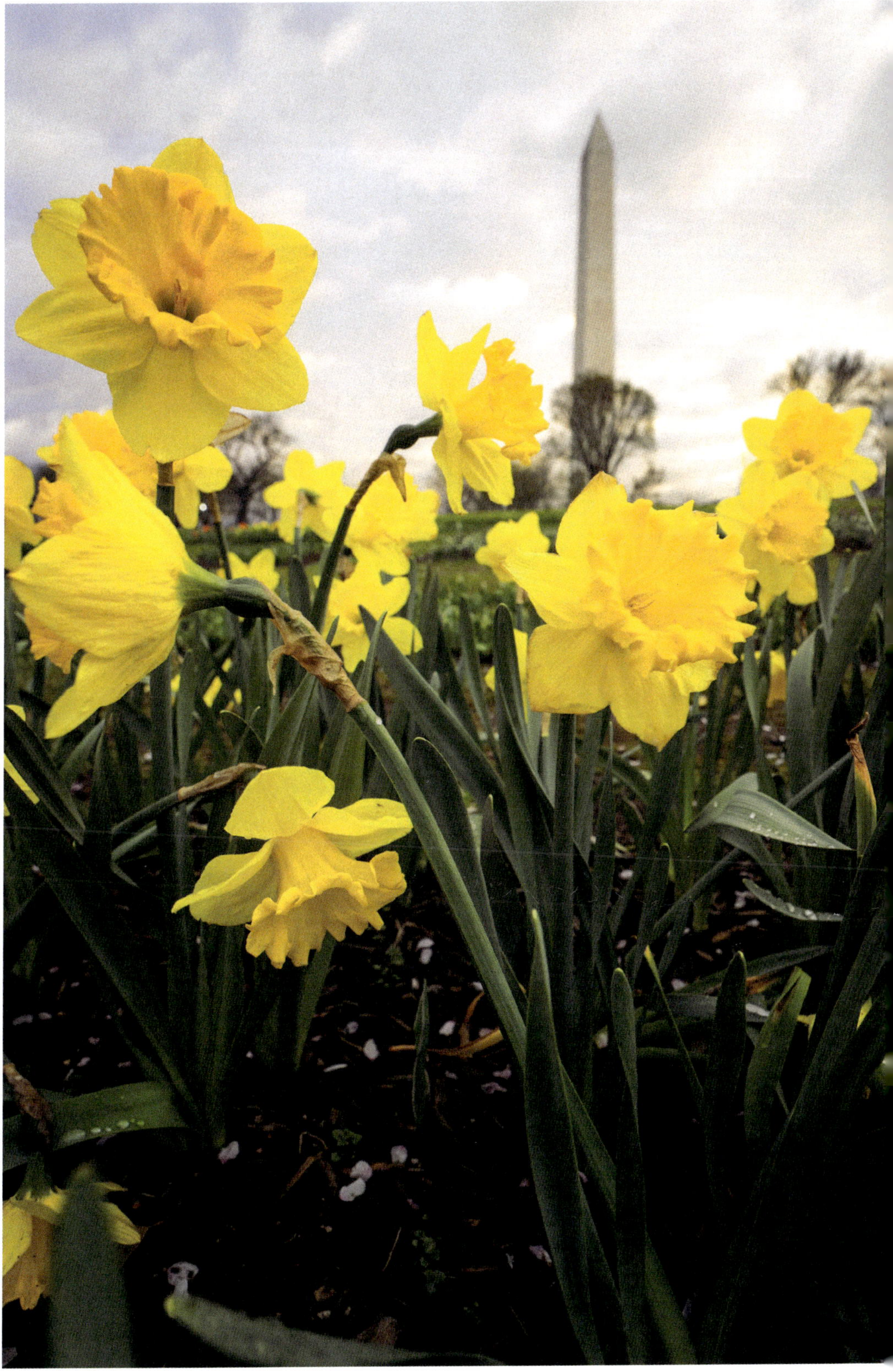

(photo on page 78)
1/60 sec F/7.1 ISO 320
Sony A7II 16-35mm

Shot in April. I'm a big fan of making foreground elements larger than the background. It's a play on perspective that is hard to see with the naked eye. To accomplish this, I usually have my camera on the ground pointing up. For this image, my camera was right at the root of these yellow daffodils.

ANGELA B. PAN	THE FLORAL LIBRARY

1/25 sec F/7.1 ISO 250
Sony A7II 16-35mm
Shot in September. The consistent pattern, leaf contrast, and rich colors make this image stand out.

1/15 sec F/6.3 ISO 100
Sony A7II 16-35mm
Shot in September, from above the flowers, with my wide-angle lens. My camera was pointed down, towards the flowers, in order to create the exaggerated shapes.

THE FLORAL LIBRARY

FAVORITE TIME OF DAY TO SHOOT:
Sunset

CLOSEST METRO:
Smithsonian

ADDRESS:
Independence Ave SW

SUGGESTED PARKING:
Tidal Basin Paddle Boat parking lot

FOR MORE INFO:
http://www.abpan.com/book/floral

the MARTIN LUTHER KING JR. MEMORIAL

Completed in 2011, the Martin Luther King, Jr. Memorial is one of our most inspiring structures in Washington. Along the perimeter of the Memorial are some of Dr. King's more famous quotes. My favorite: "Darkness cannot drive out darkness: Only light can do that. Hate cannot drive out hate: Only love can do that."

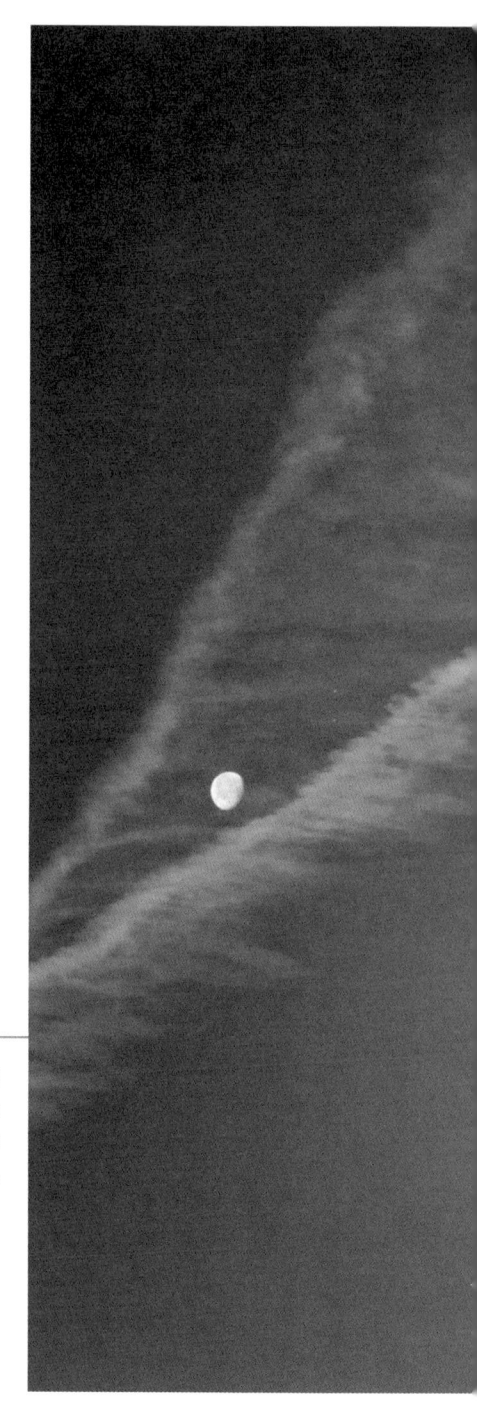

**1/80 sec F/8 ISO 100
Canon 5D Mark II 24-105mm**
The sunset light made Dr. King glow in this powerful moment.

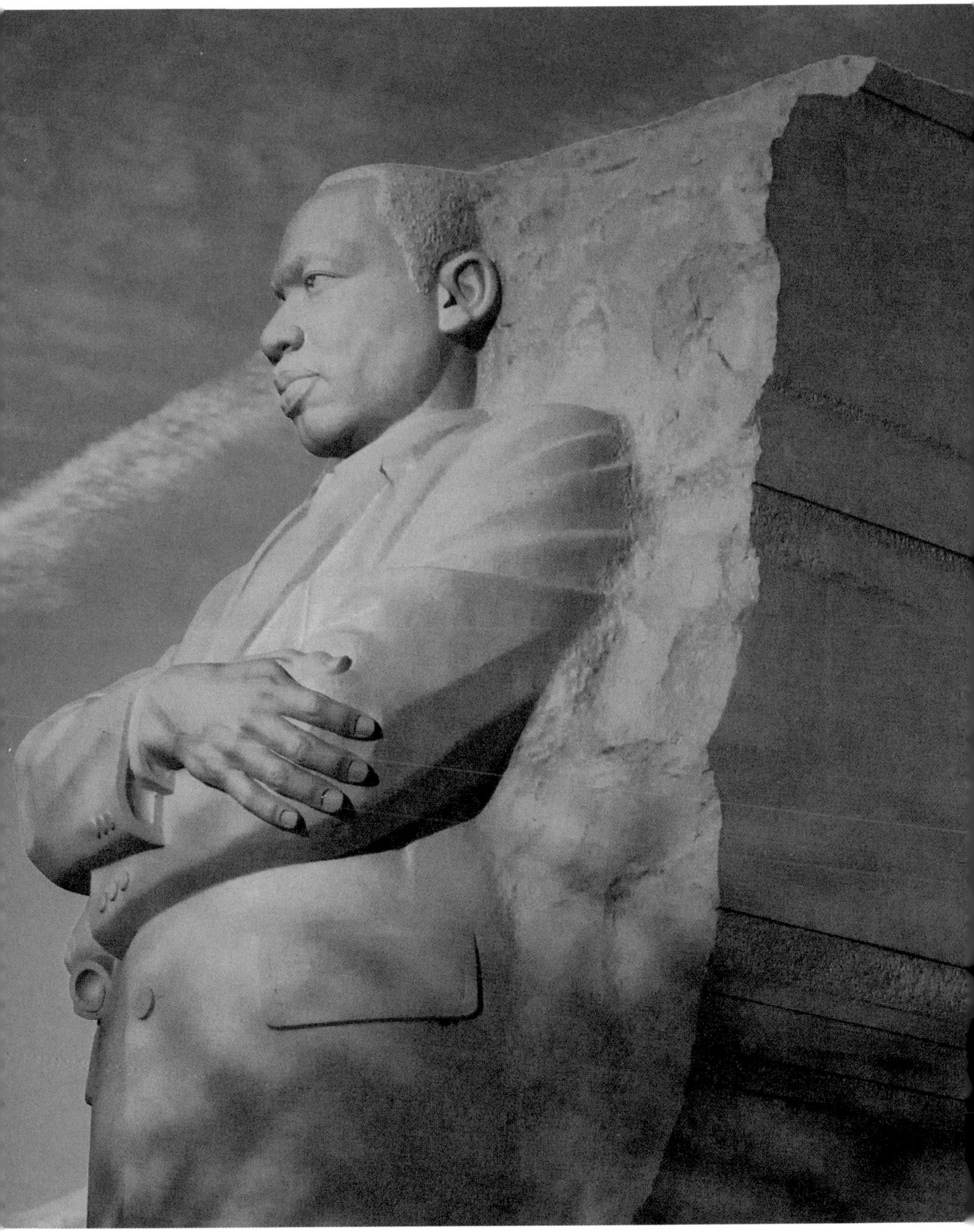

**1/25 sec F/5.6 ISO 160
Sony A7II 28/70mm**

A heart-shaped opening in the leaves created a beautiful frame for the Memorial. I was standing on a bench to capture this, which I highly recommend doing if you want to see different points of view for a potential photograph. Just be careful you're not breaking any laws, or hurting yourself, or anyone around you!

1/32 sec F/4.0 ISO 100
Canon 5D Mark II 24-105mm
This memorial can be a little more difficult to photograph if you want to give it context. The stone that Dr. King is coming out of is about one hundred feet away from the other two stones. For this image, I was practicing the "Rule of Thirds" in order to highlight Dr. King and using my zoom lens to compress the stones together.

1/125 sec F/7.1 ISO 125
Sony A7II 16-35mm

A cold winter morning at the Tidal Basin, I took advantage of the cloudless sky to create a cool toned monochromatic image. It was the silver of sunlight that shined between the two stones that brought a warm, contrasting hint and immediately made it more interesting.

THE MARTIN LUTHER KING JR. MEMORIAL

FAVORITE TIME OF DAY TO SHOOT:
Sunrise

CLOSEST METRO:
Smithsonian

ADDRESS:
1964 Independence Ave SW, Washington, DC 20024

SUGGESTED PARKING:
Ohio Dr

FOR MORE INFO:
http://www.abpan.com/book/mlkj

CHERRY BLOSSOMS

If you're lucky enough to be in the area in early springtime, you will definitely have to visit the cherry blossoms in this area. It's like you're breaking the law in D.C. if you don't! Don't get me wrong; there are more cherry blossom trees around the City. I just think the best ones grow around the Tidal Basin, especially the ones located right next to the small pedestrian footbridge (as seen on the map on page 63). There you will find really low-hanging tree branches and very twisty, turny branches.

I suggest keeping an eye out on the National Park Service (NPS) website under bloom watch.

http://www.abpan.com/book/cherryblossom

There you will find their estimated peak bloom dates, the status of the cherry blossom trees as well as a visual index of the stages the cherry blossoms go through. A great resource if you're planning your trip around the cherry blossom peak.

1/13 sec F/7.1 ISO 400
Sony A7II 100mm

The main attraction. Almost at full bloom. This particular branch was hanging over the edge of the water, so I positioned myself to use the water as a solid background to highlight the blossoms. I intentionally captured the branch coming out of the corner of the image.

ANGELA B. PAN — CHERRY BLOSSOMS

ANGELA B. PAN — CHERRY BLOSSOMS

1/4 sec F/5.0 ISO 250
Sony A7II 28-70mm

Early morning risers take it all in at Tidal Basin. Adding the photographers to the image tells the story of what it's like shooting the cherry blossoms. No matter what time of day you're at Tidal Basin, you're going to see others. Why not include them in your shot?

8.0 seconds F/5.6 ISO 200
Sony A7II 28-70mm

Cherry blossoms line the Tidal Basin around sunrise. The lights you see in between the trees are from various photographers with their cameras flashing. I can see how some people could be bothered by the extra light, but I like it. It helps tell the story. I love how the clouds are pointing to the trees so the reflection of the clouds draws the eye to a point in the center of the image.

1/200 sec F/4 ISO 320
Sony A7II 16-35mm

My intention for this shot was to catch the reflection of the people walking people past in the puddles. I had been kneeling down for awhile, and I think people were hesitant to walk in front of my lens. Once I gave them the OK, I just had to wait for that decisive moment when all the elements worked together. The secret to this was to put my camera on burst mode, take several images in quick succession, then hope for magic!

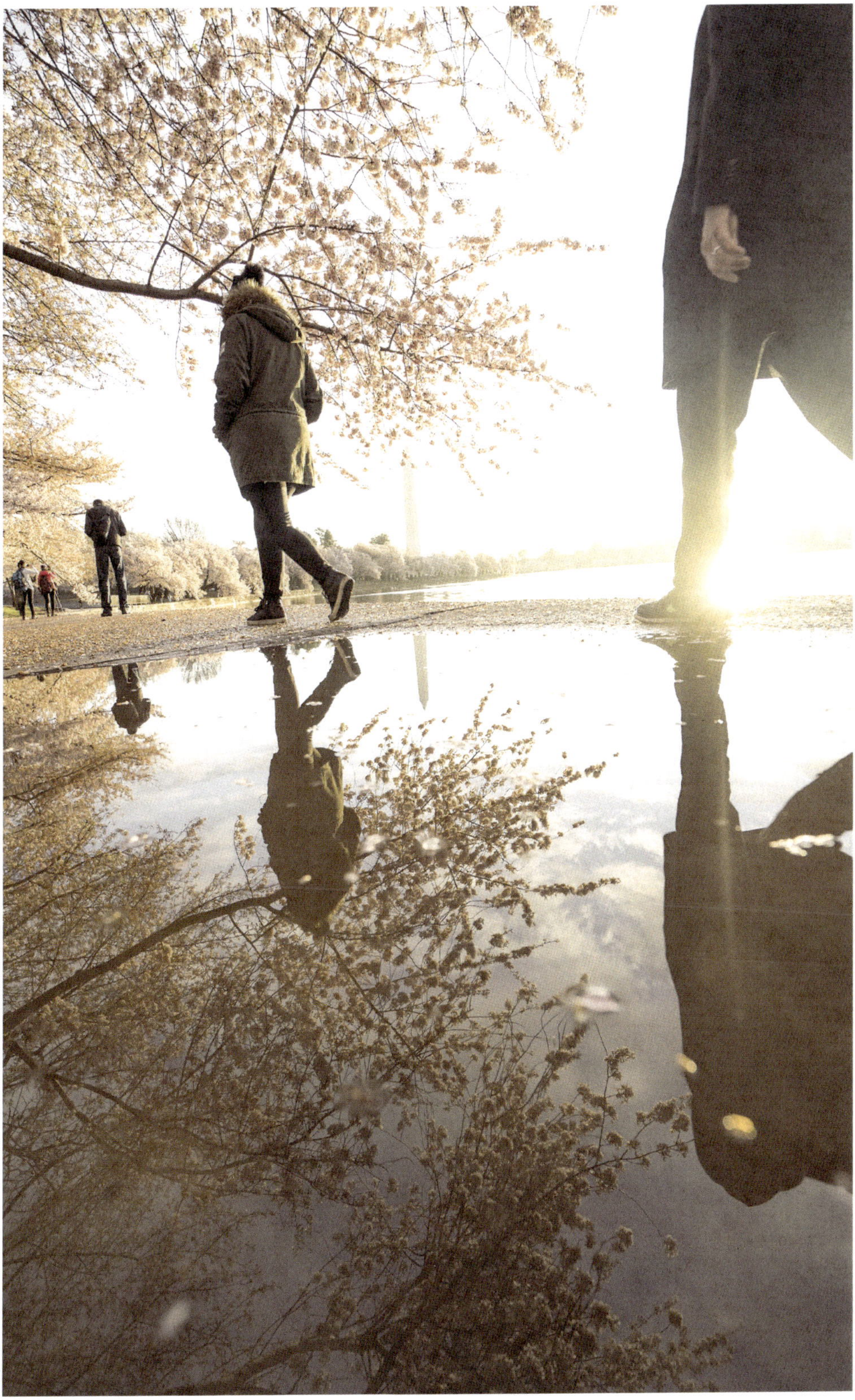

1/125 sec F/9 ISO 640
Sony A7II 16-35mm
Try taking your camera off the tripod and getting as close as you can to the flowers. You will love the framing possibilities.

(photo on pages 97-98)
1/80 sec F6.3 ISO 200
Sony A7II 28-70mm
A super foggy morning made this image possible. If it weren't for the fog, you'd probably see a lot of other cherry blossom trees in the background. Possibly the Washington Monument, too. Crazy weather conditions make for some unique, gorgeous images.

**1/100 sec F/8 ISO1000
Sony A7II 16-35mm**

Another one of those, "Take your camera off the tripod and just play with different angles," moments. Sometimes it works, sometimes it doesn't. But there's no harm in trying.

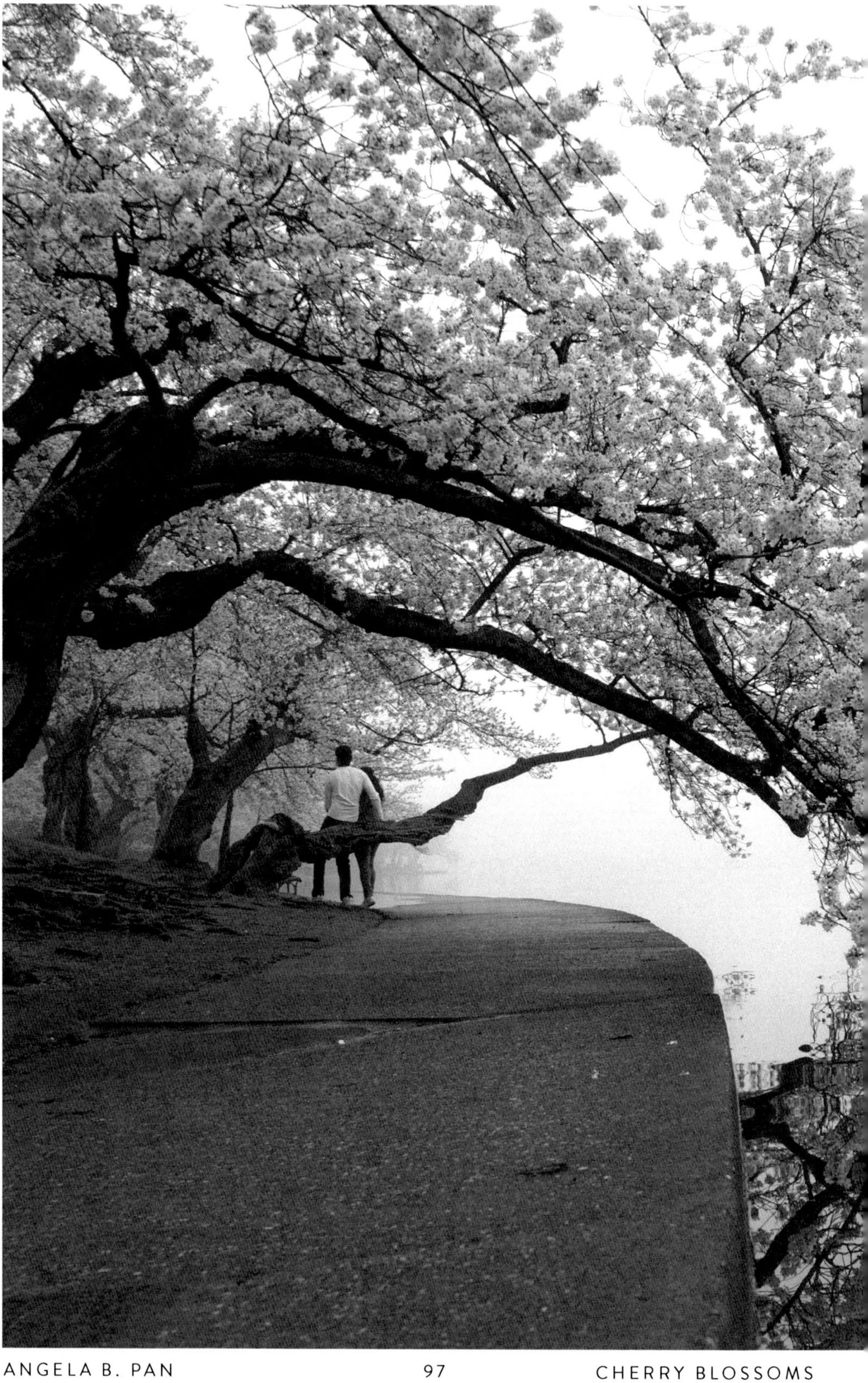

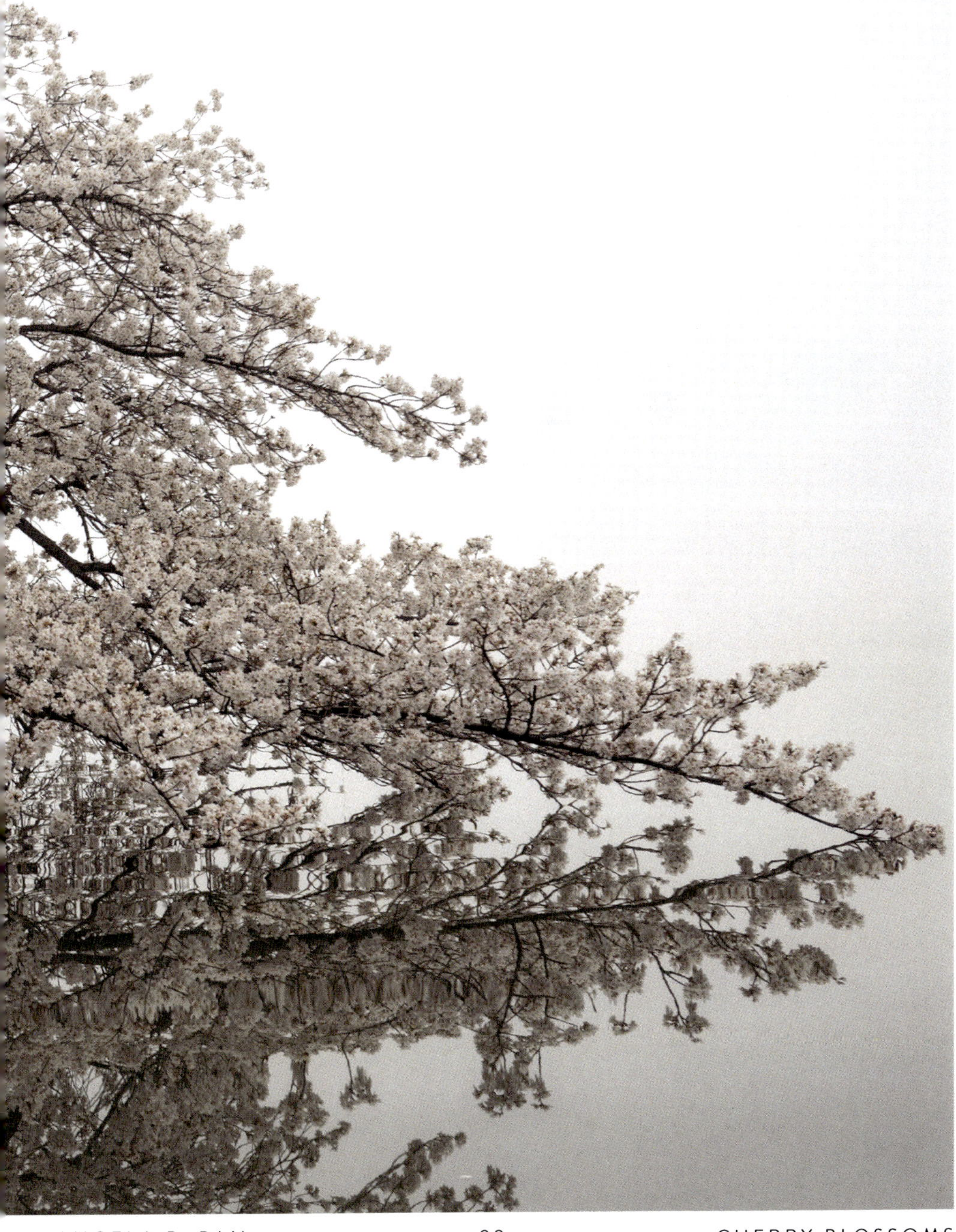

CHERRY BLOSSOMS

FAVORITE TIME OF DAY TO SHOOT:
Sunrise

CLOSEST METRO:
Smithsonian

ADDRESS:
1500 Maine Ave SW, Washington, DC 20024

SUGGESTED PARKING:
Ohio Dr, Park A

FOR MORE INFO:
http://www.abpan.com/book/cherryblossom

FALL AT THE BASIN IS AWESOME TOO...

1/5 sec F/5.6 ISO 125
Sony A7II 16-35mm

Another foggy morning. Using a single element like the park bench will invite your viewer to take an even closer look. It's sort of like adding a human element.

KUTZ BRIDGE

It's a secret spot only locals know about, because it's not that obvious when you're just casually walking past. Located across Independence Ave, it is a little section blocked off from the rest of the Tidal Basin. But once you see it, you'll know what I'm talking about. It's like a little Tidal Basin, all to itself.

ANGELA B. PAN — KUTZ BRIDGE

(photo on pages 101-102)
1/30 sec F/4.5 ISO 200
Sony A7II 28-70mm

Black and white images should be reduced down to basic elements. My favorite elements to look for are shapes and lines.

1.3 seconds F/5.6 ISO 250
Sony A7II 28-70mm

Sunrise, facing east, waiting for the sun to rise at the edge of the water. If it weren't for the street lights on the right-hand side to balance the Washington Monument on the left, the image would definitely be off-kilter.

This is also another great go-to spot to photograph the cherry blossoms. You'll get all the same great qualities of the real Tidal Basin, but it definitely won't be as crowded.

1.3 seconds F/11 ISO 80
Sony A7II 16-35mm

**2.0 seconds F/14 ISO 200
Sony A7II 28-70mm**

Foggy morning at the bridge. With a line that extends into nothing, I made sure the lights from either side of the image weren't colliding with each other, making the bridge appear even longer than its true length.

KUTZ BRIDGE

FAVORITE TIME OF DAY TO SHOOT:
Sunrise

CLOSEST METRO:
Smithsonian

ADDRESS:
Kutz Bridge Washington, DC 20024

SUGGESTED PARKING:
Tidal Basin Paddle Boats parking lot

FOR MORE INFO:
http://www.abpan.com/book/kutz

Constitution Gardens

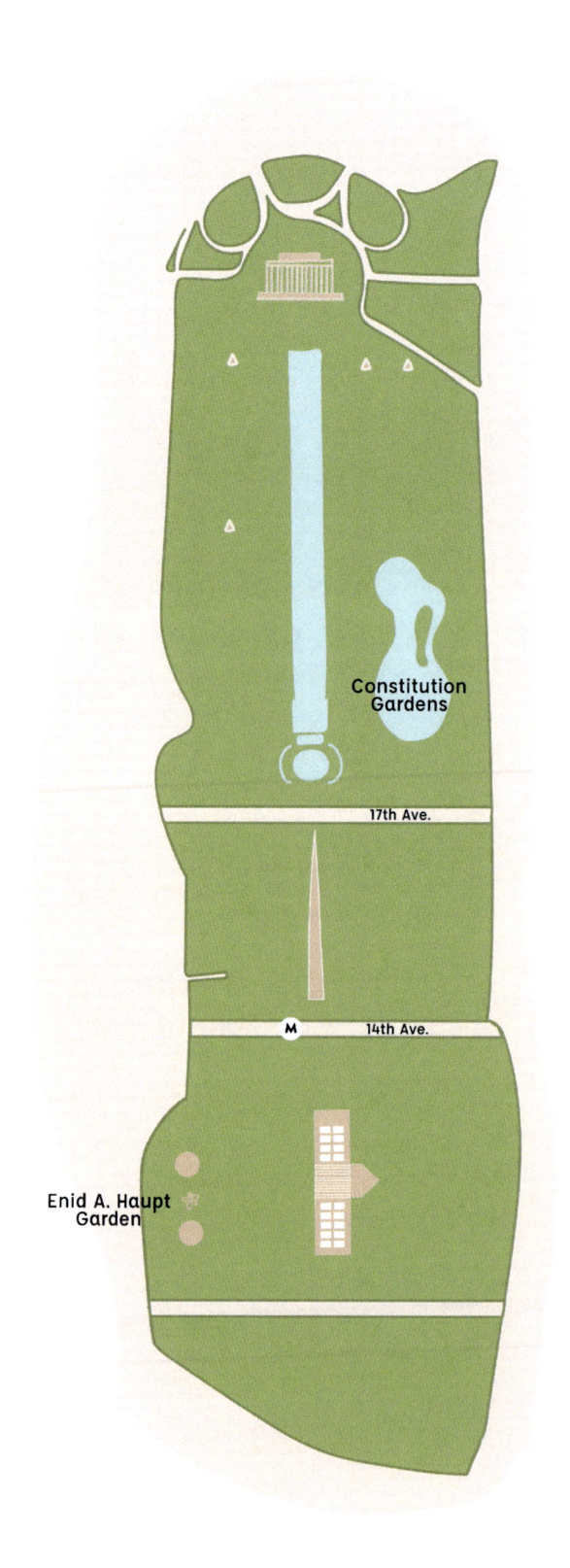

17th Ave.

14th Ave.

Enid A. Haupt Garden

MEMORIAL GARDENS

MEMORIAL GARDENS

If you think about a city, especially Washington, D.C., you might not think about nature or gardens at first. But we actually have quite a few. And they're so beautiful! They are such great places to meet up with friends or even to go for a lunchtime walk. These are a few of my favorites around the National Mall.

Other gardens to consider visiting: United States Botanical Gardens (and don't forget Bartholdi Park, right next door), National Art Gallery Sculpture Garden, Hirshhorn Museum and Sculpture Garden, Kenilworth Park and Aquatic Gardens.

1/8 sec F/6.3 ISO 200
Sony A7II 28-70mm
Using the edge of the pond to divide the image into two separate parts--the water and ducks, versus the concrete and trees. This combines two different textures and creates more interest in the image.

CONSTITUTION GARDENS

Adjacent to the National World War II Memorial is this beautiful, quiet garden. It may be because it is hidden behind the trees, but most of the time I am the only one there. My favorite time of year to visit this garden is in the fall. I love seeing the leaves change and drop to the ground.

2.0 seconds F/5.6 ISO 400
Canon 5D Mark II 24-105mm

It also has these amazing willow trees branches that I love to watch blow in the wind.

**1 1/80 sec F/6.3 ISO 400
Sony A7II 16-35mm**

Although they aren't the most obvious element here, the birds add interest to this photo through line and repetition, which helps lead your eye from left to right. I also think their reflection in the water is cool.

CONSTITUTION GARDENS

FAVORITE TIME OF DAY TO SHOOT:
Sunrise

CLOSEST METRO:
Farragut West

ADDRESS:
1850 Constitution Ave. NW (U.S. Highway 50), Washington D.C.

SUGGESTED PARKING:
Constitution Ave

FOR MORE INFO:
http://www.abpan.com/book/constitutiongardens

ENID A. HAUPT GARDENS

This garden really comes alive in the springtime with its beautiful magnolia trees, cherry blossom trees, and tulips. But even if you're not visiting in the spring, the Enid A Haupt Garden is a great place to take a short walk in any season. There's so much to see in the garden, with access points to smaller galleries such as the Arthur M. Sackler Gallery, an Asian-influenced art museum, and the National Museum of African Art. It's located right behind the Smithsonian Castle, with several entrances accessible from the National Mall or Independence Ave.

1/160 sec F/4.0 ISO 200
Sony A7II 16-35mm

Looking up in the gardens, my eyes keep following the branches and the different layers the magnolias create from the bottom up.

ANGELA B. PAN — ENID A. HAUPT GARDENS

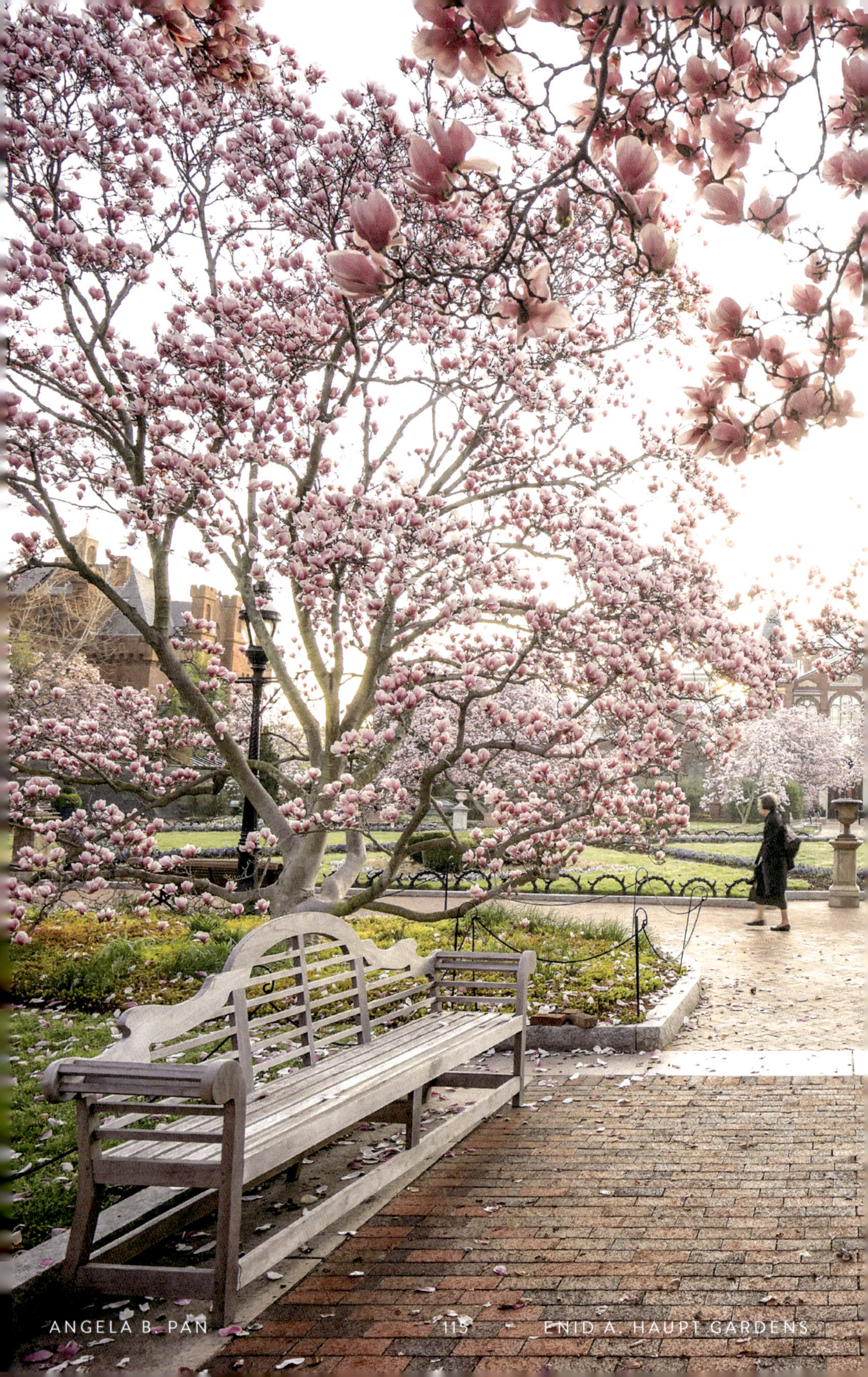

ANGELA B. PAN — ENID A. HAUPT GARDENS

(photo on pages 115-116)
1/50 sec F/7.1 ISO 200
Sony A7II 16-35mm
Shot right outside the Moongate Garden entrance. Everything is in perfect symmetry, besides the person walking past. It's that little off-balance element that makes the image even more interesting.

1/1250 sec F/5.6 ISO 320
Sony A7II 28-70mm
View of the Washington Monument from the east entrance on Independence Ave. The magnolia trees made for a perfect frame for the "pencil".

ENID A. HAUPT GARDEN

FAVORITE TIME OF DAY TO SHOOT:
Early Morning

CLOSEST METRO:
Smithsonian

ADDRESS:
12 Independence Ave SW, Washington, DC 20219

SUGGESTED PARKING:
Independence Ave, Jefferson Dr SW, Madison Dr NW

FOR MORE INFO:
http://www.abpan.com/book/hauptgarden

GOVERNMENT BUILDINGS

the WHITE HOUSE

The White House and The US Capitol are so close that they often get confused as being a part of the National Mall. However, these government buildings are not. They are maintained as they own but they are so close that they should not be missed.

A difficult place to photograph in the past couple of years, since security has become much stricter at the White House. It has gotten to the point where you can't even stand next to the fence. You have to stand across the street of the South Lawn if you want to see the building. No tripods are permitted. Tons of security. Tons of people.

However, it's still on the "Do-Not-Miss" list. Not only do you have amazing views of the Washington Monument and the Jefferson Memorial from here, but the coolest part is seeing helicopters taking off or landing right on the South Lawn. Is that the President? I don't know! It's so hard to see from across the street. Plus, it's the White House, so you gotta go see it!

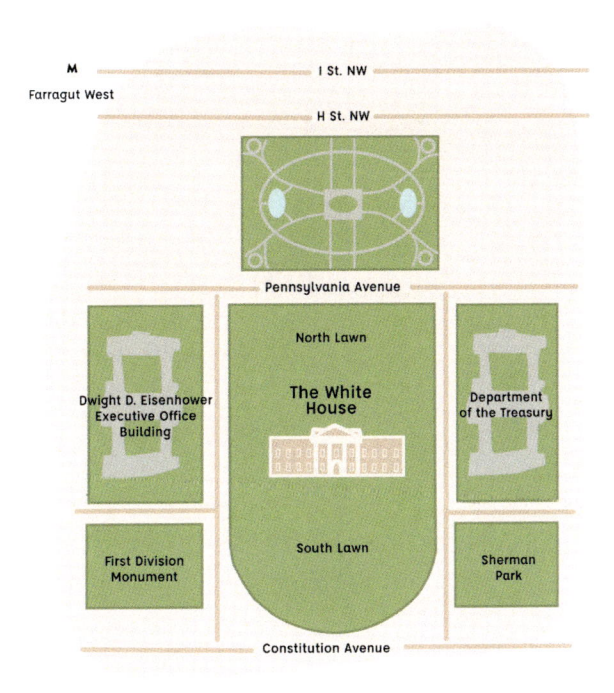

**1/2 sec F/11 ISO 100
Canon 5D Mark II 24-105mm**

This is an image of the sunrise, facing south. It may be a little easier to capture since you can get a little bit closer to the fence.

**1/200 sec F/6.3 ISO 320
Sony A7II 70-200mm**
View from south side from across the street.

ANGELA B. PAN · THE WHITE HOUSE

THE WHITE HOUSE

FAVORITE TIME OF DAY TO SHOOT:
Sunset

CLOSEST METRO:
Farragut West Metro

ADDRESS:
1600 Pennsylvania Ave NW, Washington, DC 20500

SUGGESTED PARKING:
Pennsylvania Ave

FOR MORE INFO:
http://www.abpan.com/book/whitehouse

the UNITED STATES CAPITOL BUILDING

Also known as the Capitol, this building is one of the best places in the District to capture a dramatic sky. It doesn't matter if you're there at sunrise or at sunset, you can get great images. If you have a long zoom lens, this is a great place to use it. There are so many great details in the architecture of the building that you may not be able to see without it. I usually come here with the intention of capturing interesting reflections and surface details.

The best time of year to go is in late summer, when Congress isn't in session. It's almost eerie how few people are around the grounds at this time.

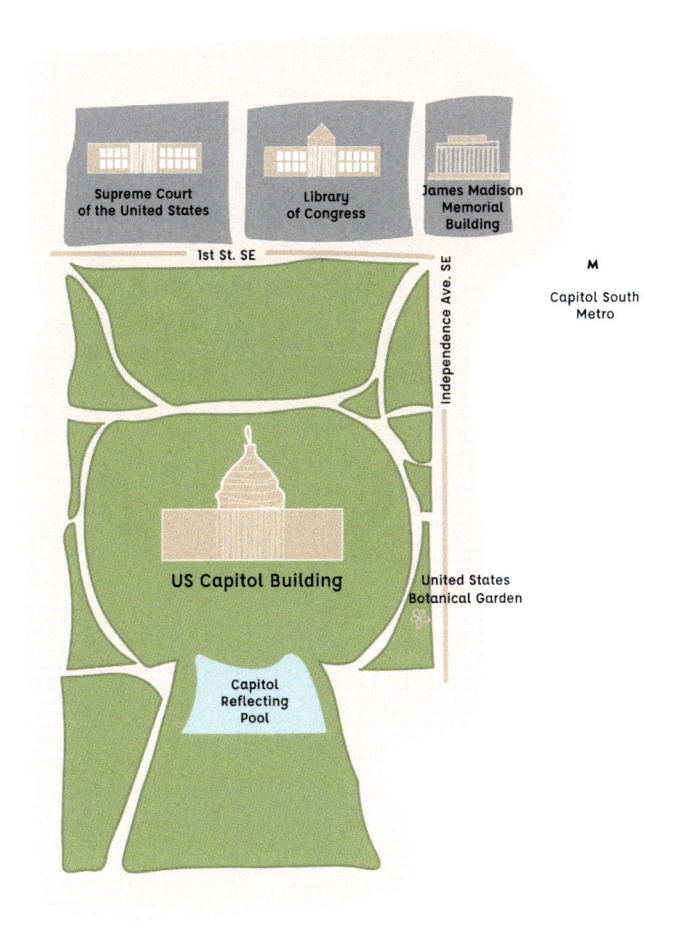

**1/100 sec F/6.4 ISO 320
Canon 5D Mark II 70-200mm**
An example of what you can capture with a great zoom lens. Here, I was zoomed in all the way at 200mm.

30 seconds F/7.1 ISO 2500
Sony A7II 16-35mm
Sunrise image, facing east at the Capitol Reflecting Pool. The long exposure with my neutral density filter made the water appear even smoother than it really was.

ANGELA B. PAN — THE CAPITOL BUILDING

ANGELA B. PAN   128   THE CAPITOL BUILDING

1/160 sec F/6.3 ISO 320
Sony A7II 16-35mm

Catch some of the best rainbows at the U.S. Capitol. Somehow, they always line up right above the dome. By now you should know that I love taking pictures right after it rains or snows. Bad weather doesn't stop me from doing what I love. My favorite thing to do after it rains is look for puddles and see what reflections I can get out of them. My camera was hovering right over the puddle to find the third rainbow in this image. The double yellow lines also help lead you through this image.

ANGELA B. PAN — THE CAPITOL BUILDING

(photo on pages 127-128)
5 seconds F/10 ISO 100
Canon 5D Mark II 17-40mm
Dusk, facing east side of the building.

1/15 sec F/6.3 ISO 320
Sony A7II 16-35mm
Sunset at the Capitol Reflecting Pool, facing west. The ducks created some amazing lines while swimming in the water. You'll want to use these kinds of elements to your advantage.

**30 seconds F/4 ISO 800
Sony A7II 16-35mm**
Another long exposure to make the clouds in the background softer and the water look still.

ANGELA B. PAN　　　　　131　　　　　THE CAPITOL BUILDING

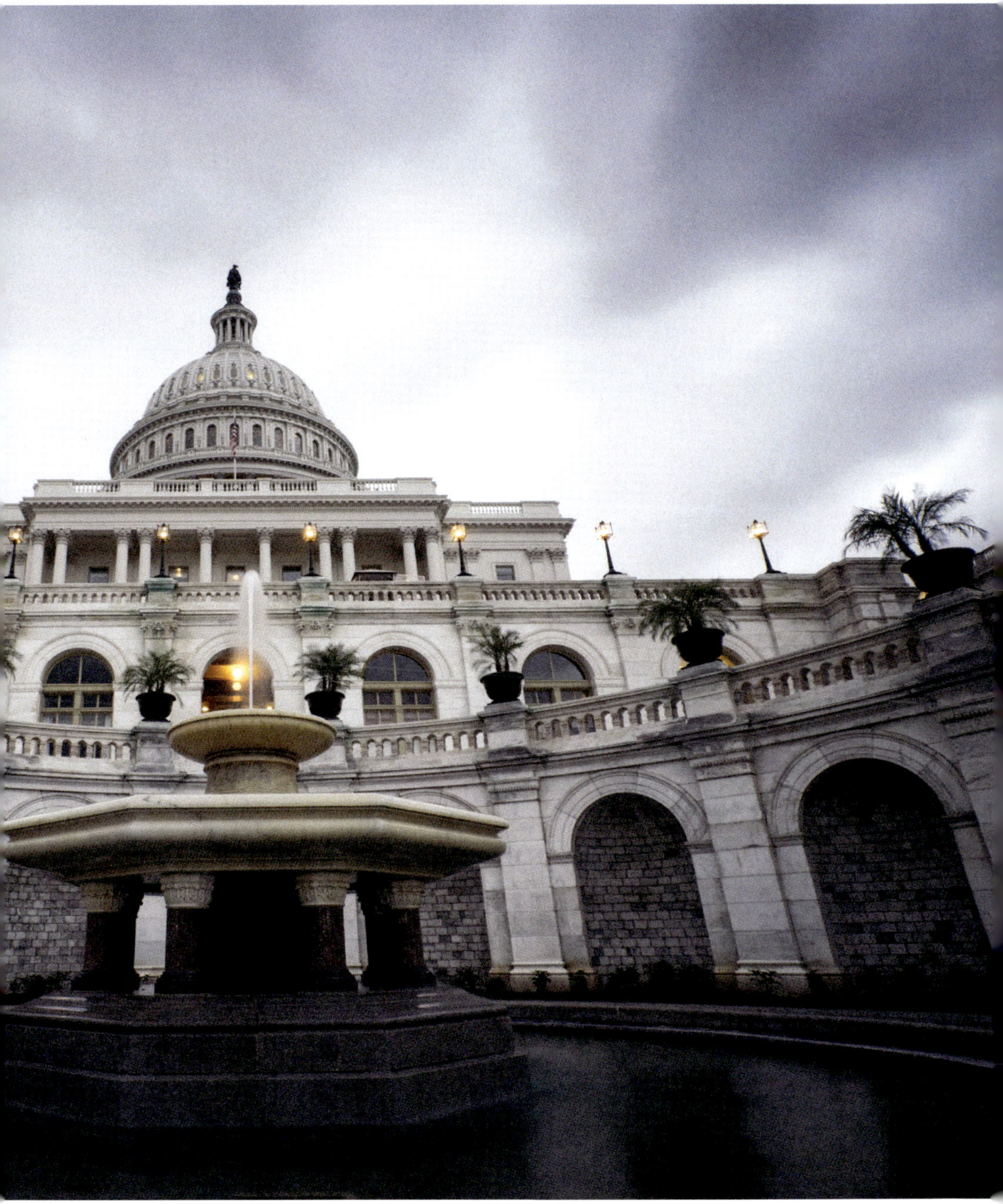

Inside The Capitol

I highly recommend going on the free Capitol tour. You can book it in advance online or, if you're lucky, you may get same-day tickets. The tour takes about an hour and is highly informative.

**1/50 sec F/7.1 ISO 3200
Canon 5D Mark II 17-40mm**

Try to get to the Capitol as early in the day as possible. Not only will it be less crowded, but hopefully you'll get some good light coming through the dome windows for your photographs.

ANGELA B. PAN   134   THE CAPITOL BUILDING

1/13 sec F/7.1 ISO 3200
Canon 5D Mark II 17-40mm
I'm using the "Rule of Thirds" to capture this image, vertically and horizontally.

1/15 sec F/4.5 ISO 500
Sony A7II 28-70mm

The curtain makes for the perfect frame behind this statesman in the statue room.

ANGELA B. PAN   136   THE CAPITOL BUILDING

**1/200 sec F/4.5 ISO 2500
Sony A7II 16-35mm**
This room is pretty dark, despite the windows on top. I suggest bumping up your ISO, which will make the shutter faster to ensure you get everything in sharp focus.

ANGELA B. PAN THE CAPITOL BUILDING

THE UNITED STATES CAPITOL BUILDING

FAVORITE TIME OF DAY TO SHOOT:
Sunset

CLOSEST METRO:
Capitol South

ADDRESS:
East Capitol St NE & First St SE, Washington, DC 20004

SUGGESTED PARKING:
3rd St NW, E Capitol St NE

FOR MORE INFO:
http://www.abpan.com/book/capitol

LIBRARY *of* CONGRESS

Not even lying, the Library of Congress contains my favorite interior in all of Washington. You just have to trust me! It's absolutely gorgeous. I don't know how anyone could get any reading, studying, or anything else done here. I feel like I'd just be looking up at the ceiling the entire time I was there.

Since it's located right across the street from the U.S. Capitol, I recommend taking the Capitol Tour, then walking the underground tunnel from here to the Library of Congress. It's a lot faster than walking across the street, you avoid getting checked by security twice, and how often do you get to walk in an underground tunnel?

1/50 sec F5.6 ISO 250
Sony A7II 16-35mm

A random hallway in the Library of Congress. It was the light from the windows on the left that really drew my eye to this scene. It added that extra element of light and reflection to the gleaming floor.

ANGELA B. PAN · LIBRARY OF CONGRESS

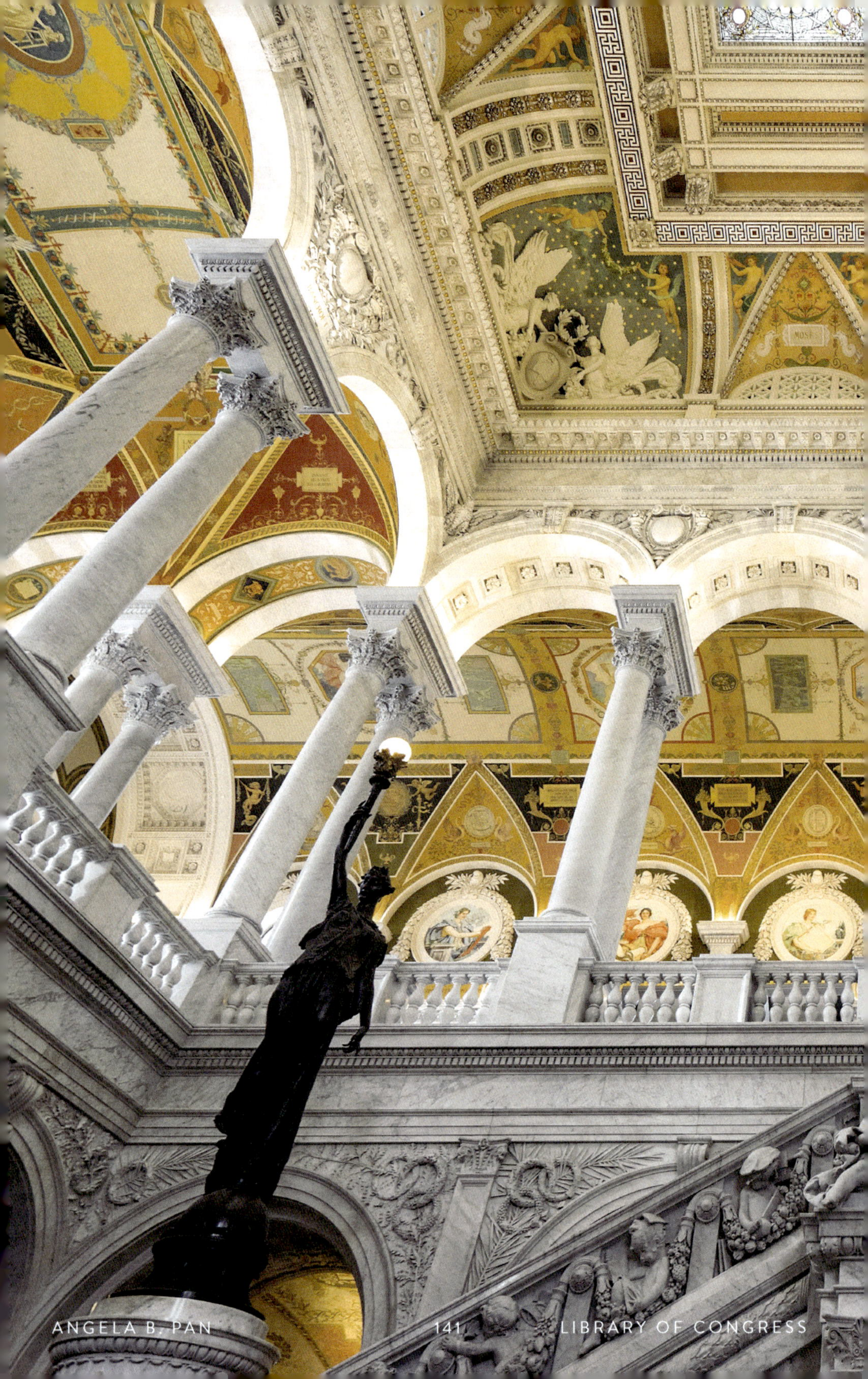

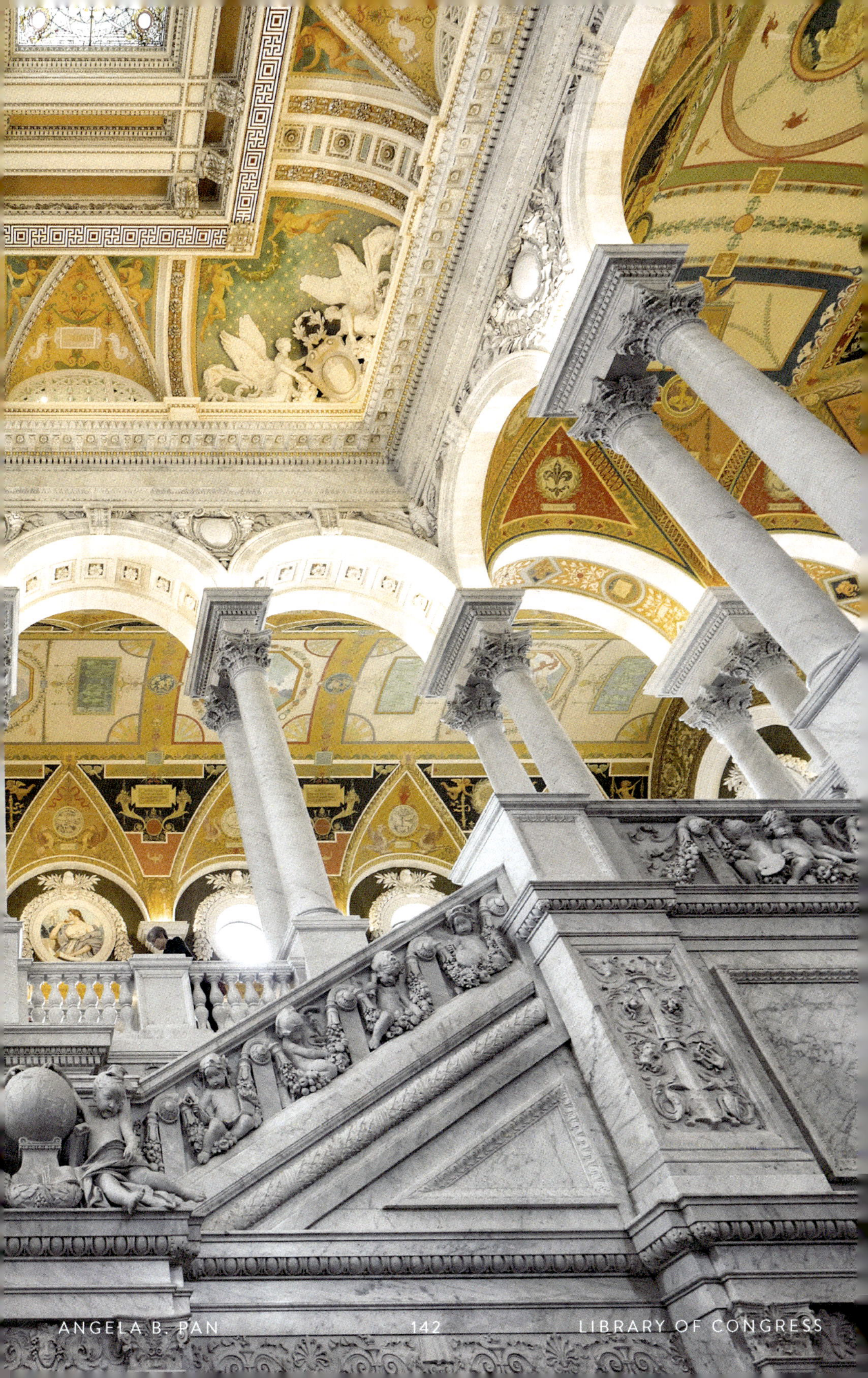

(photo on pages 141-142)
1/15 sec F/6.3 ISO 1000
Sony A7II 16-35mm

A wide-angle lens is your best friend in the Library of Congress. You'll want to capture as much of the internal environment as possible.

1/8 sec F/5.6 ISO 250
Sony A7II 16-35mm

The Main Reading Room opens to the public only twice a year: Presidents Day and Columbus Day. If you're in the D.C. area at that time, make sure to arrive at the Library right when it opens. It fills up with visitors very quickly!

the JAMES MADISON MEMORIAL BUILDING

This is part of the Library of Congress, but my favorite viewpoint of it is definitely its exterior. The columns and lines outside of it create such cool depth and pattern.

LIBRARY OF CONGRESS & THE JAMES MADISON MEMORIAL

FAVORITE TIME OF DAY TO SHOOT:
Anytime

CLOSEST METRO:
Capitol South

ADDRESS:
101 Independence Ave SE, Washington, DC 20540

SUGGESTED PARKING:
E Capitol St NE

FOR MORE INFO:
http://www.abpan.com/book/loc

1/640 sec F/7.1 ISO 500
Sony A7II 16-35mm
That's my puppy, Frankie! My favorite model.

FAVORITE PLACES OUTSIDE
of the
NATIONAL MALL

FAVORITE PLACES OUTSIDE *of* *the* NATIONAL MALL

I've concentrated most of the information in this book on the National Mall. It's a beautiful place to visit, and there's just so much to see in its 146 acres. But that's not the end of it. There's so much more to see in the rest of the city and surrounding areas. Some of the places are:

- Union Station *149*
- Arlington Memorial Bridge *155*
- The United States Marine Corps War Memorial *162*
- Netherlands Carillon *167*
- The United States Air Force Memorial *172*
- The United States Arboretum *181*
- Rock Creek Park *188*
- Great Falls National Park and Scott's Run Nature Preserve *193*

UNION STATION

I don't know, you may think it's a little strange that I picked a transit station as one of my favorite places to shoot, but it is! The architecture inside and outside is just breathtaking.

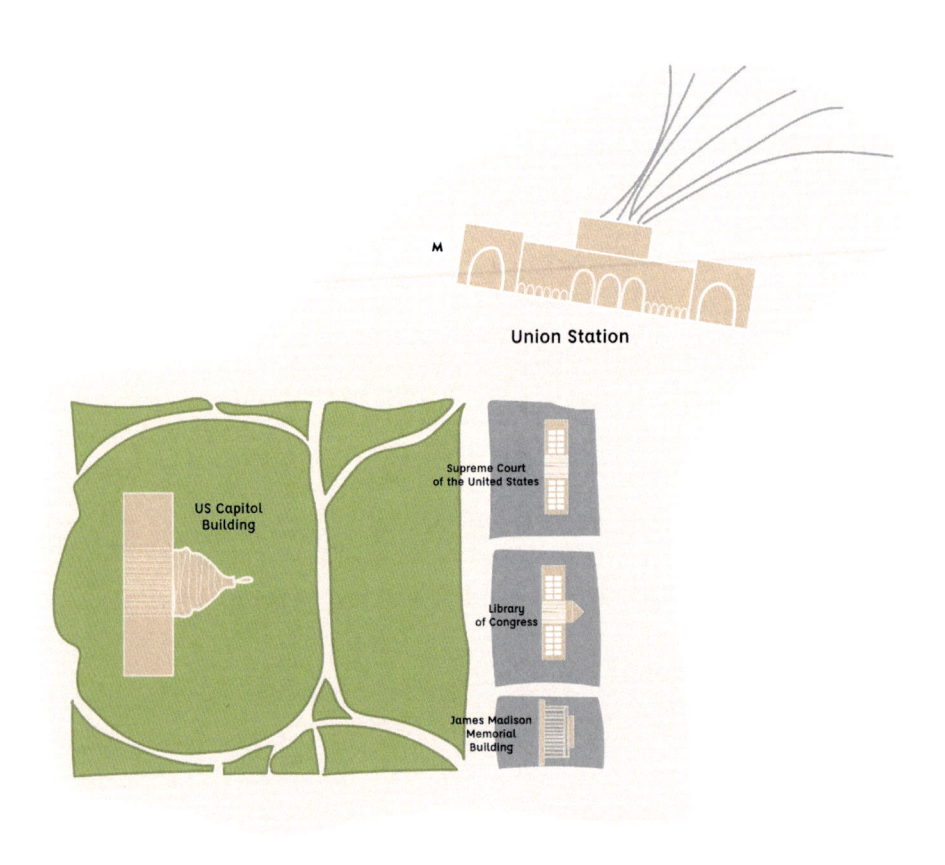

1/50 sec F/7.1 ISO 200
Canon 5D Mark II 17-40mm

The fountain in front of Union Station. The line these birds in formation creates gives your eye an upward direction to follow in this image.

1/4 sec F/11 ISO 1000
Canon 5D Mark II 17-40mm
Gazing up at Union Station, you can see the ceiling is amazing.

1/25 sec F/6.3 ISO 640
Canon 5D Mark II 17-40mm
As you're walking in the front entrance, check out the view on the right. The walkway is rich with repetition, pattern, and line.

1/5 sec F/10 ISO 160
Sony A7II 28-70mm

From the top of the parking garage, you can get some cool views of the US Capitol. Walk to the other side of the parking lot and you'll see train tracks. If you're there at an especially busy time, a long exposure with car light trails could look very cool here.

ANGELA B. PAN 153 UNION STATION

UNION STATION

FAVORITE TIME OF DAY TO SHOOT:
Sunset

CLOSEST METRO:
Union Station

ADDRESS:
50 Massachusetts Ave NE, Washington, DC 20002

SUGGESTED PARKING:
Union Station parking garage

FOR MORE INFO:
http://www.abpan.com/book/unionstation

ARLINGTON MEMORIAL BRIDGE
- On The Virginia Side -

The bridge is one of the only places you'll get views of the Lincoln Memorial and Washington Monument from a distance. Walk a little bit further and you'll see the Jefferson Memorial too.

You can either walk across the Memorial Bridge from D.C. or drive into Virginia and park your car at the Theodore Roosevelt Island parking lot.

1/60 sec F/6.3 ISO 160
Sony A7II 28-70mm

This image was taken from the walk from Theodore Roosevelt Island. If you choose to park your car here, the trail splits into two paths. Stay towards the left on the trail closest to the water. The other way will have you walking next to the highway.

**1.0 second F/5.6 ISO 160
Canon 5D Mark II 70-200mm**

Along side of the Memorial Bridge is a fantastic place to catch the fireworks on the Fourth of July. My favorite part about this location is seeing the color variations in the water. A nearly impossible capture from inside the Mall.

1 second F/5.6 ISO 160
Canon 5D Mark II 70-200mm

Even though it's a more zoomed-in look, you'll want to choose what is your main focus. In this particular image, it's the smoke and fireworks that held my attention.

1 second F/22 ISO 200
Canon 5D Mark II 24-105mm
Spring is a great time to see daffodils and tulips in the city.

ANGELA B. PAN — MEMORIAL BRIDGE

1/40 sec F/8 ISO 160
Sony A7II 28-70mm

A fall morning, using colorful leaves to frame the monuments in a different way. Compositions like this aren't obvious. I stood on top of a hill on my tippy toes to capture this, making sure the leaves and the memorials looked like they were almost touching. It created great depth, so the time and effort was worth it.

ANGELA B. PAN   MEMORIAL BRIDGE

ARLINGTON MEMORIAL BRIDGE

FAVORITE TIME OF DAY TO SHOOT:
Surise

CLOSEST METRO:
Rosslyn

ADDRESS:
Northbound lanes of the George Washington Parkway between Roosevelt Bridge and Key Bridge Arlington, VA 22209

SUGGESTED PARKING:
Theodore Roosevelt Island parking lot

FOR MORE INFO:
http://www.abpan.com/book/memorialbridge

the UNITED STATES MARINE CORPS WAR MEMORIAL

Just outside of Washington in Arlington, Virginia, is the Iwo Jima Memorial and the Netherlands Carillon.

This is one of the only places you'll get views of the three main landmarks: The Lincoln Memorial, the Washington Monument, and the U.S. Capitol Building.

1.0 second F/5.6 ISO 125
Canon 5D Mark II 24-105mm

Iwo Jima is another great place to watch the Fourth of July fireworks, but it can be busier than downtown. The fireworks can be seen from so many points of view, with a lot of open space, but if you do decide to go here, go as early as possible. One year I heard a guy here say he'd been waiting for the fireworks to begin since 9 a.m. You probably won't have to arrive that early, but definitely come early, and pack some snacks. You can see a little bit of the Washington Monument behind the first soldier on the right.

ANGELA B. PAN · MARINE CORPS MEMORIAL

**1/13 sec F/22 ISO 100
Canon 5D Mark II 24-105mm**
Sunrise, facing east. I was super excited when I saw this sky. The small clouds, repeated in these lines, really brought the focus down to the Iwo Jima Memorial and flag.

ANGELA B. PAN — MARINE CORPS MEMORIAL

1/15 sec F/5.6 ISO 640
Sony A7II 16-35mm
Taken during a break in the rain. The gradient from dark to light in the top portion of the image brings all the drama and interest to other areas of the image.

ANGELA B. PAN — MARINE CORPS MEMORIAL

1 second F/22 ISO 64
Sony A7II 16-35mm
This is my second favorite place to catch a rainbow after it rains, and especially to capture color contrast. The warm, orangish red clouds are cut off by the rainbow, which then leads into the cool-toned sky. This can really color an image with emotion.

NETHERLANDS CARILLON

Walking distance to the Marine Corps Memorial is the Netherlands Carillon. The Carillon itself isn't much to see, though it's pretty to hear its music. For now, I just use it as a point of reference for a beautiful flower display and a great view of the D.C. monuments. In the past, you were even able to climb to the very top, though not anymore.

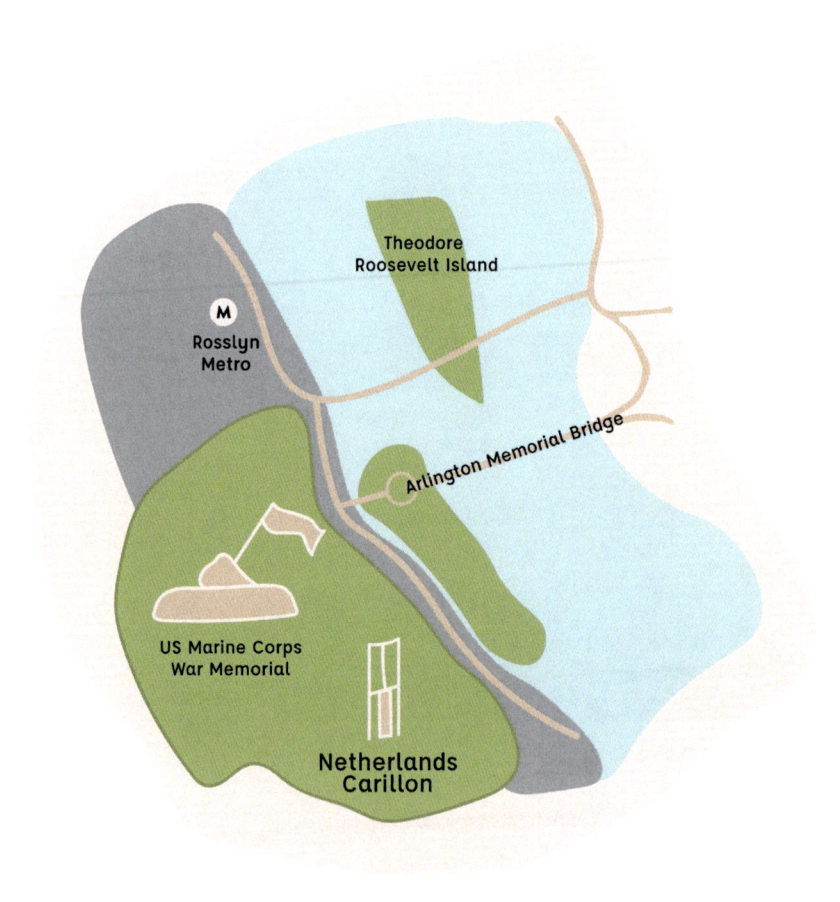

ANGELA B. PAN — NETHERLANDS CARILLON

page 168)
ISO 80
16-35mm

Washington landmarks from Netherlands Carillon with the pretty flowers as foreground.

1/30 sec F/5.0 ISO 2500
Sony A7II 70-200mm

A great place to watch the full moon rise and one of the only places to capture all three memorials in one image. The bigger the zoom, the better!

ANGELA B. PAN — NETHERLANDS CARILLON

(photo on page 170)
1/15 sec F/8 ISO 160
Sony A7II 16-35mm
Focusing on foreground elements to make them larger than life, and a play on perspective with my camera on the ground.

UNITED STATES MARINE CORPS WAR MEMORIAL & NETHERLANDS CARILLON

FAVORITE TIME OF DAY TO SHOOT:
Surise

CLOSEST METRO:
Rosslyn

ADDRESS:
1400 North Meade St, Arlington, VA.

SUGGESTED PARKING:
Iwo Jima Memorial Access Rd

FOR MORE INFO:
http://www.abpan.com/book/iwojima

the UNITED STATES AIR FORCE MEMORIAL

Also located in Arlington, Virginia, the Air Force Memorial honors personnel who have served in the Air Force and its heritage organizations. At 270 feet, this memorial can be a little difficult to photograph in a single shot. My advice for shooting here is to walk around the Memorial, even exiting the main area to check out some street-level views of it. I've included what it looks like from the side, and even from outside the Memorial grounds.

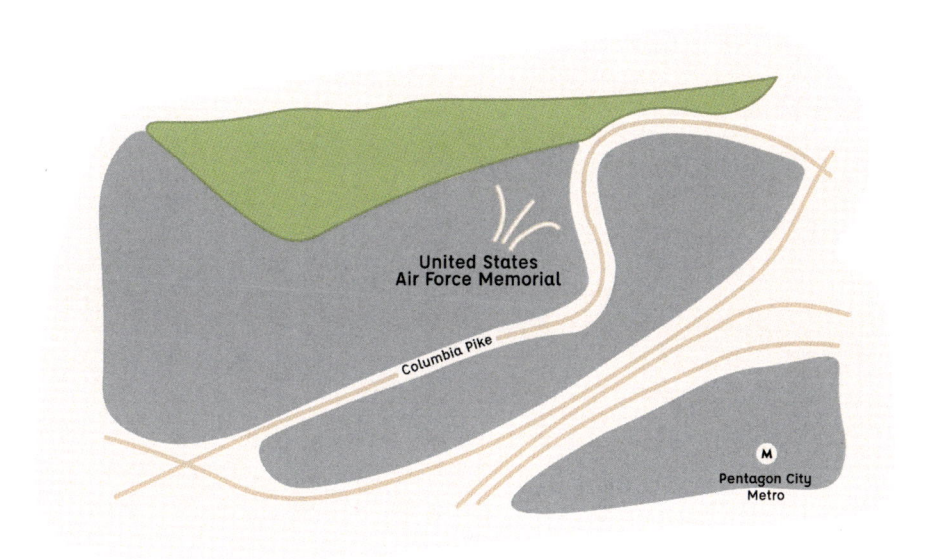

**1/6 sec F/10 ISO 250
Canon 5D Mark II 17-40mm**
You see that little, itty-bitty, stick-looking thing in the background? That's the Washington Monument!

ANGELA B. PAN — AIR FORCE MEMORIAL

1/60 sec F/3.5 ISO 400
Sony A7II 28-70mm
Sitting on the hill just outside the Memorial, using the dandelions as foreground elements.

ANGELA B. PAN — AIR FORCE MEMORIAL

ANGELA B. PAN — AIR FORCE MEMORIAL

1/5 sec F/9 ISO 200
Canon 5D Mark II 17-40mm
The view from Columbia Pike, with the Memorial perfectly centered.

1/100 sec F/7.1 ISO 1250
Canon 5D Mark II 24-105mm
A mid-winter sunrise, facing southeast from the corner viewing area. Taken from inside the grounds.

ANGELA B. PAN — AIR FORCE MEMORIAL

ANGELA B. PAN — AIR FORCE MEMORIAL

ANGELA B. PAN   AIR FORCE MEMORIAL

1/15 sec F/5.6 ISO 400
Sony A7II 70-200mm
Lightning strike close to the Jefferson Memorial, seen from the hill right outside the United States Air Force Memorial. Although I used my zoom lens to capture this, I cropped it even further in photoshop in order to really focus in on the main subject: the lightning bolt. The Capitol Building can be seen from this spot, as well.

(photo on pages 177-178)
1/250 sec F/5.6 ISO 160
Sony A7II 16-35mm

Looking up from the center of the base of the Air Force Memorial as a storm was about to hit. This Memorial isn't as iconic as the others, so it's easier to come up with new compositions without being influenced by the vision of others.

THE UNITED STATES AIR FORCE MEMORIAL

FAVORITE TIME OF DAY TO SHOOT:
Sunset

CLOSEST METRO:
Pentagon City

ADDRESS:
1 Air Force Memorial Dr, Arlington, VA 22204

SUGGESTED PARKING:
Parking at the memorial

FOR MORE INFO:
http://www.abpan.com/book/airforce

the UNITED STATES NATIONAL ARBORETUM

A beautiful botanical garden with the National Capitol columns as its centerpiece. Located in Northeast D.C., it's a little ways out of the action compared to the National Mall, but a great place to spend time with your family and camera. These columns used to be part of the U.S. Capitol, but were relocated to the Arboretum in 1958.

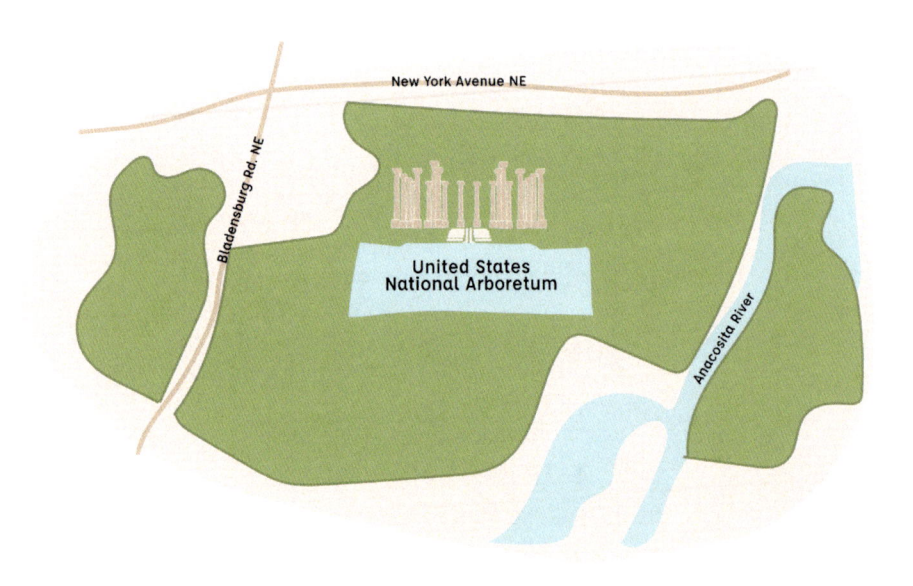

1/500 sec F/5.6 ISO 100
Sony A7II 16-35mm
Wildflowers used as foreground and the main subject of this image. It still provides the context of your location, without being too obvious.

ANGELA B. PAN — US NAT'L ARBORETUM

1/25 sec F/22 ISO 100
Sony A7II 16-35mm
Taken in the middle of the day, using the shadows of the columns to create lines to the sun starburst.

ANGELA B. PAN — US NAT'L ARBORETUM

1/30 sec F/9 ISO 64
Sony A7II 16-35mm
Taken close to sunset on a crisp autumn afternoon, the water feature makes for a great place to capture interesting reflections.

1/1250 sec F/5.6 ISO 100
Sony A7II 16-35mm
My favorite part of the Arboretum is the Bonsai tree collection. So little, but so cute! Again, using shadows to create extra lines and interest in this image.

ANGELA B. PAN · US NAT'L ARBORETUM

1/200 sec F/6.3 ISO 100
Sony A7II 16-35mm

THE UNITED STATES NATIONAL ARBORETUM

FAVORITE TIME OF DAY TO SHOOT:
Afternoon - Sunset

CLOSEST METRO:
Not convenient to Metro. The closest Metrorail subway stop is Stadium Armory Station on the Blue and Orange lines. Transfer to the B2 Metrobus; disembark the bus on Bladensburg Road at R and Street, just past the Arboretum sign on the right. Walk back to sign at R Street and walk down R Street two blocks to Arboretum entrance.

ADDRESS:
3501 New York Ave NE, Washington, DC 20002

SUGGESTED PARKING:
Parking lot at the Arboretum

FOR MORE INFO:
http://www.abpan.com/book/arboretum

ROCK CREEK PARK

If I didn't live in the Washington area, I would have assumed that Rock Creek Park was super-dangerous. From its depiction in TV shows, like House of Cards, to movies, like Enemy of the State, it seems like the place to meet when you want to do something dangerous or illegal. But it's far from that! With thirty-two miles of hiking trails, it's an outstanding getaway from busy city life.

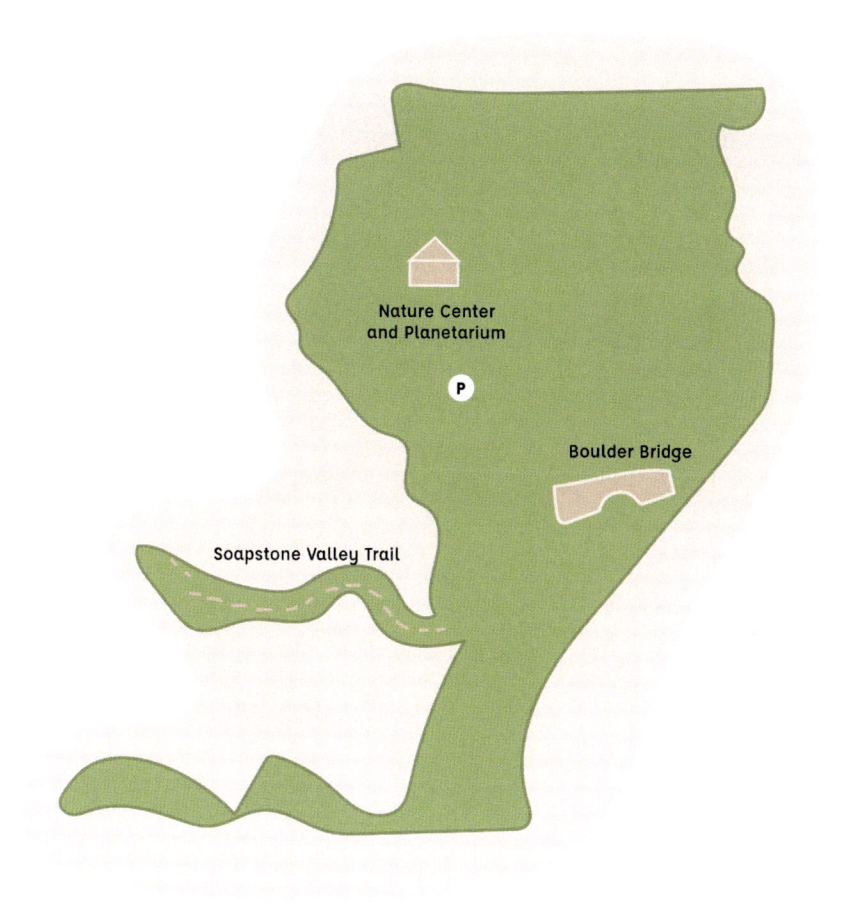

1/2 sec F/7.1 ISO 200
Sony A7II 16-35mm
Rock Creek Park is so colorful in autumn. This image was taken at Boulder Bridge, shot with camera low to the ground to capture the best reflections.

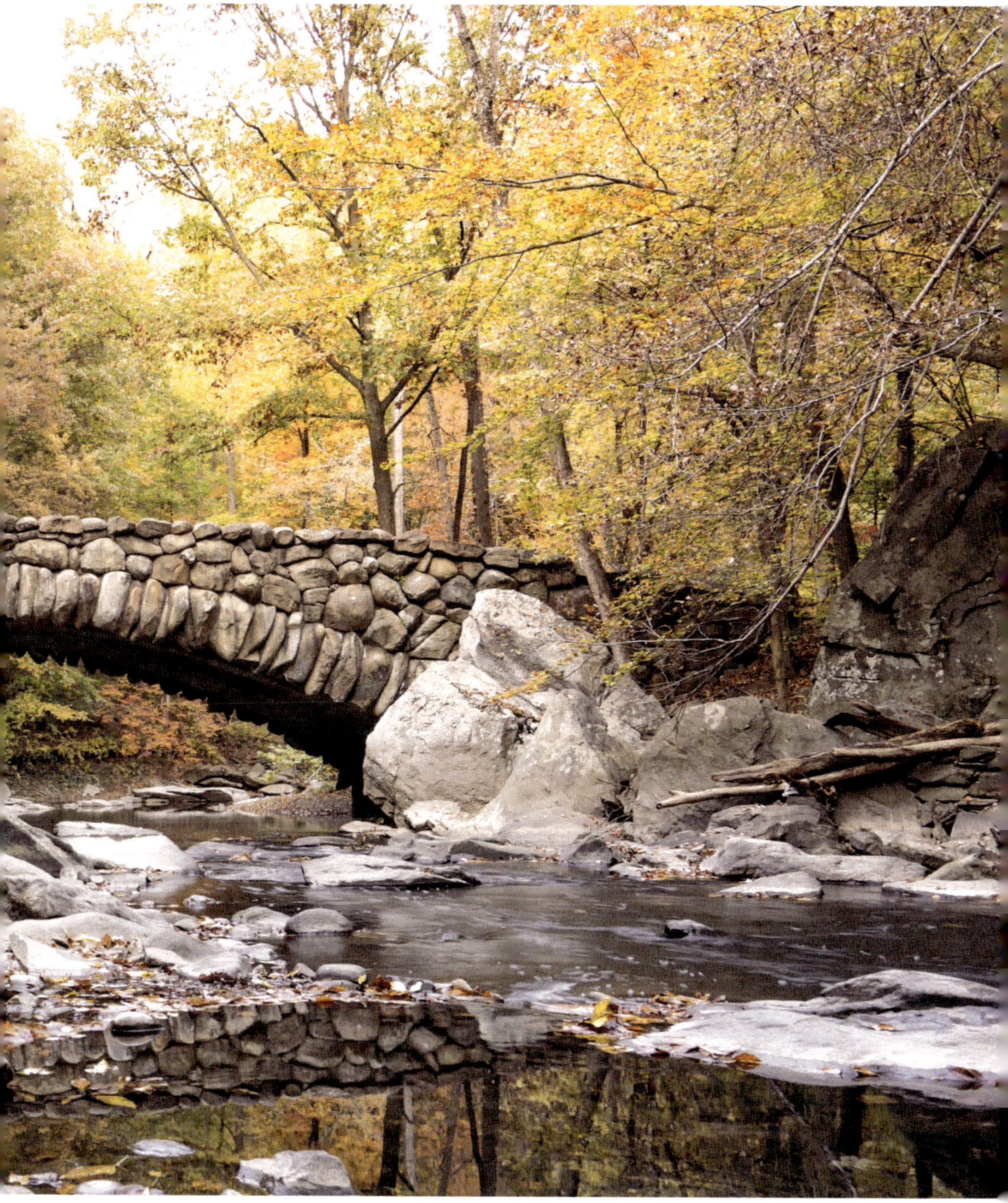

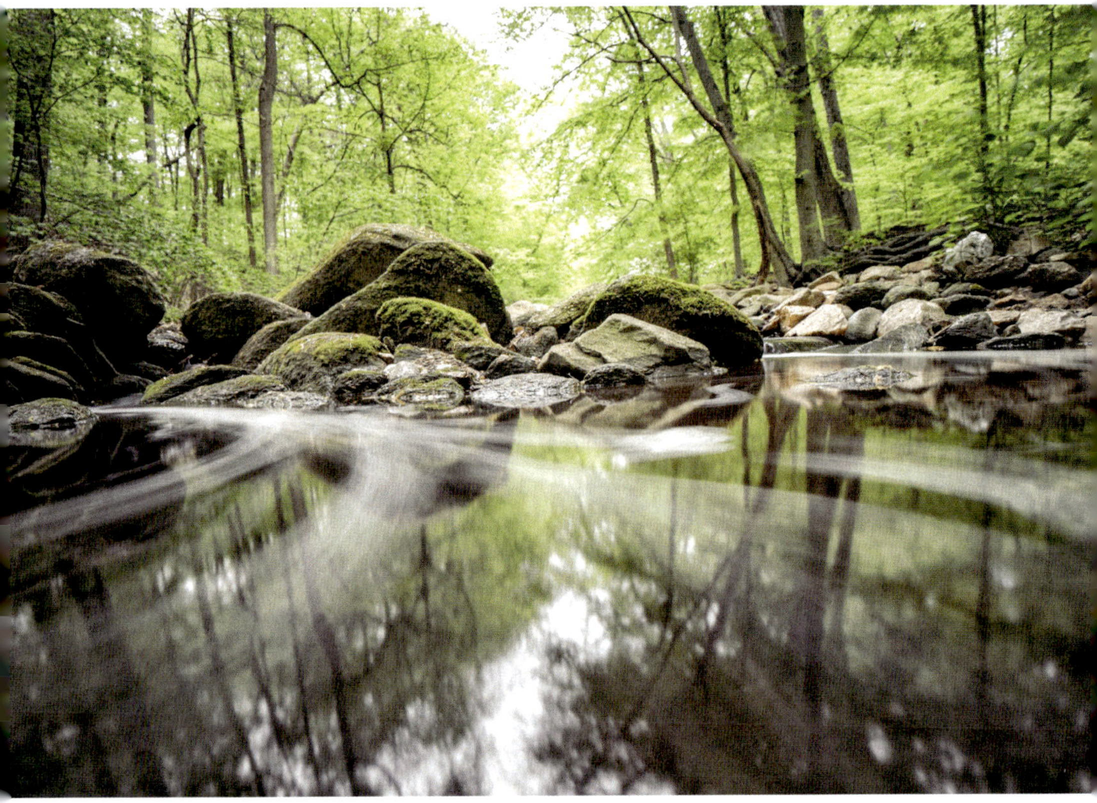

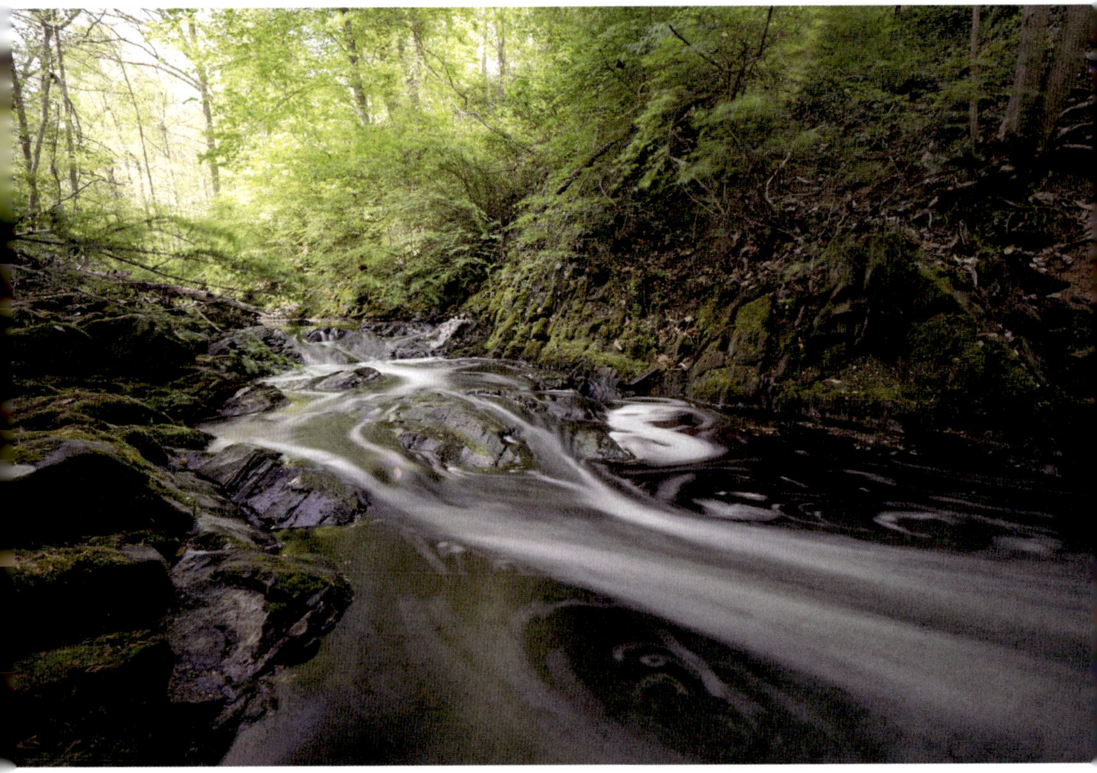

13 seconds F/5.0 ISO 640
Sony A7II 16-35mm

Soapstone Valley Trail in Rock Creek Park. I shot this with my 10-stop neutral density filter in the middle of the day, while balancing on some rocks. I took this during a photowalk with @igdc, a great Instagram community of amazing Washington-area photographers.

ROCK CREEK PARK

FAVORITE TIME OF DAY TO SHOOT:
Sunset

CLOSEST METRO:
To the Nature Center: Take the metro to Friendship Heights Metro Station and then take the bus to the Military + Glover stop

ADDRESS:
To the Nature Center: 5200 Glover Road, NW, Washington, D.C.

SUGGESTED PARKING:
Parking at the Nature Center

FOR MORE INFO:
http://www.abpan.com/book/rockcreek

10 seconds F/5.6 ISO 640
Sony A7II 16-35mm

A long exposure created the white "flow" of the water, which makes for great leading lines.

GREAT FALLS NATIONAL PARK *and* SCOTT'S RUN NATURE PRESERVE

And, if you have finished your tour of my favorite D.C. landmarks, here's a bonus: Just outside of Washington is my favorite place to shoot nature.

Great Falls National Park and Scott's Run Nature Preserve

There are no metro or bus stops near Great Falls. You'll either have to drive or find a ride to it somehow, but it's totally worth it. This National Park is just twenty miles outside of the city but you would never know it. You're in your own little world when you come to Great Falls Park.

There is a Maryland side to Great Falls, and a Virginia side. You'll get better views of the waterfall on the Virginia side, but the Maryland side is great for hiking trails. If I had to choose between the two, I'd go with Virginia.

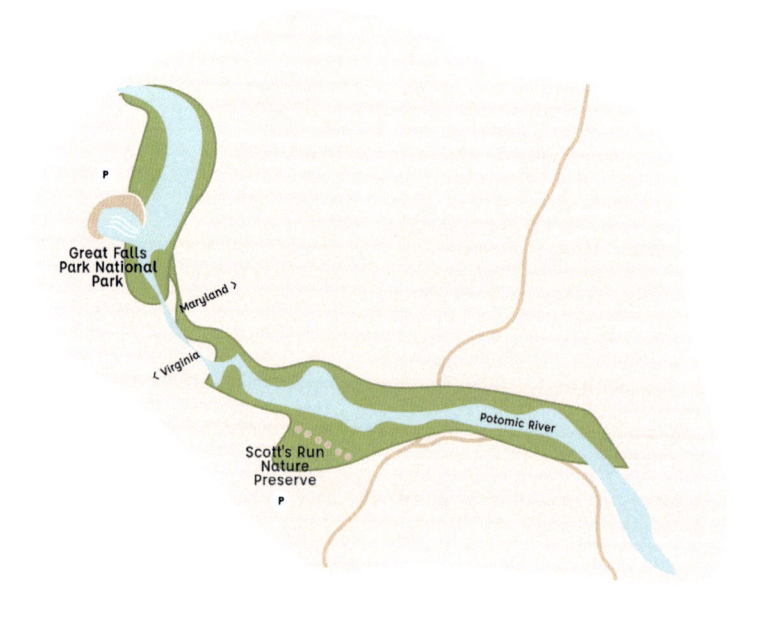

GREAT FALLS NATIONAL PARK
- On The Virginia Side -

1/8 sec F/8 ISO 200
Canon 5D Mark II 17-40mm
Winter morning at sunrise.

1/2 sec F/4.0 ISO 125
Canon 5D Mark II 24-105mm
Great place to see blue herons. Just bring your zoom lens.

8.0 seconds F/22 ISO 100
Canon 5D Mark II 24-105mm
A closer up look at some of the rocks and water of Great Falls Park.

10 seconds F/6.3 ISO 320
Sony A7II 16-35mm
Taken from outlook #1. I used my neutral-density filter to slow down the shutter speed in order to make the water look smooth.

1/2 sec F/18 ISO 50
Sony A7II 16-35mm
Sunset, from the Virginia side, facing Maryland. The white line in the center divides the image vertically, while the "Rule of Thirds" is applied horizontally. The sunset made the trees glow this beautiful orange color.

SCOTT'S RUN NATURE PRESERVE

Just down the Potomac River from Great Falls Park, Scott's Run Nature Preserve is a great place for a hike and perfect for shooting fall foliage.

1/60 sec F/6.3 ISO 125
Sony A7II 16-35mm
Looking up, all the tree lines pointing to the center create a great natural circle.

1 second F/18 ISO 125
Sony A7II 16-35mm
At the end of the trail, you'll hit this little waterfall. Makes for a great reward after the hike.

GREAT FALLS NATIONAL PARK & SCOTT'S RUN

NATURE PRESERVE
FAVORITE TIME OF DAY TO SHOOT:
Sunset

CLOSEST METRO:
5 miles from Greensboro or Spring Hill Metro stops

ADDRESS:
9200 Old Dominion Dr, McLean, VA 22102

SUGGESTED PARKING:
Great Falls Park parking lot, Scotts Run parking lot

FOR MORE INFO:
http://www.abpan.com/book/greatfalls

CONCLUSION

That's it! All the secrets I've learned from shooting photographs in the Washington, D.C., area. I said I love many different places depicted in this book, and it's really true. Each location holds a special place in my heart. I never tire of shooting this wonderful city, and I hope the same will be true for you now, too!

Thank you so much for taking the time to look at my work. I hope you enjoy it and that my passion and excitement for photography jump out from these images.

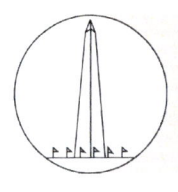

If you participated in the Washington Monument game, how many times did you see it appear in the book? The correct answer is....37.

If you're interested in sample travel itineraries, please download them at http://www.abpan.com/book/.

If there's something you didn't see in the book that you'd like to see covered in the future, or if you have any additional comments or questions, feel free to contact me through my website.

Also, if you used any of my advice to take your own pictures, I'd love to see your results. Tag me on Facebook, Instagram, or Twitter @abpanphoto and use #snapdc.

To see even more of my photography, watch my vlogs, or to purchase prints, check out: www.abpan.com/

Finally, all my photography gear is listed on my site: www.abpan.com/my-gear

ACKNOWLEDGMENTS

Shout out to you, dear reader. Thank you so much for taking time to discover this book! You may or may not know me personally, but you now have a piece of my heart. I hope you found this work informative, fun, and beautiful.

Special thanks to my husband, Andrew, who is my Number One support system. You are the person who encourages me daily to follow my dreams and pushes me to be the best person I can be. I love you, boo.

My parents, who have been there for me no matter what, even when I quit my stable job to pursue a creative profession. You didn't like it, and even told me you didn't like it, but you were always there for me. Thank you. I love you both so much.

To my grandparents, brother, aunts, uncles, cousins, in-laws, nephews, and nieces. You all put a smile on my face, and have given me so many great memories that can't be replaced.

To the Fab 5! You made me the person I am today. I would never have as much confidence, happiness, or as many embarrassing stories as I do if it weren't for you guys. Muah!

To my friends, thank you for being you. Every day I feel your energy cheering me on.

My Internet friends, your unconditional support means the world to me. If given the opportunity, I'd love to give each one of you a gigantic hug and a high five. You are the coolest of the cool.

Special thanks to the National Park Service for everything that you do to maintain and keep the National Mall as beautiful as it is.

And last but not least, the people who helped make this book possible:

Anelise Salvo, for being the awesomest graphic designer ever.
Andrew, Alejandra, Rick, Frithjov, and Eric for reading and re-reading my words. I'm extremely grateful for your patience and kindness.

To Albert, Paul, and Birch for your time, support, and friendship.

ABOUT *the* AUTHOR

As a full-time professional photographer since 2012, Angela B. Pan says she wouldn't trade her career for any other. From a first-year photography class in high school, throughout two decades of developing her own photographic vision of the world, Angela's skillful craftsmanship and unique framing of nature and architectural subjects have inspired dozens others.

"Even a four o-clock wake-up alarm, calling me to spend time with the sunrise, doesn't bother me at all," Angela says. "I wake up each day with such passion."

The author of *SNAP DC, Your Guide to Taking Extraordinary Photos of the National Mall and Beyond*, Angela's first published volume of photographs and insights for the lay and professional picture-taker, Angela has worked with industry leaders Lionsgate, Apple, The Washington Post, Rosewood Escapes, Loews Hotels, Kaiser Permanente, and The White House Historical Association, among others, to craft dynamic images in print. Her photography has been licensed for use in multiple products and services and exhibited in gallery settings. She was voted "Best Visual Artist" in Washington, D.C., by the Washington City Paper.

"Instead of using the analog camera, I'm now using my DSLR and Photoshop as my main tools of the trade," says Angela. "But I feel fortunate to have found my passion at an early age."

When not scouting out a location to set up her tripod for a photo shoot after a rainstorm in the Washington, D.C. area, she makes her life with her "favorite model," Frankie, husband, Andrew, and family in Virginia. Angela can otherwise be found watching puppy videos, eating french fries, or shopping online.

Follow Angela on her current social networks:

FACEBOOK.COM/ABPANPHOTO
INSTAGRAM.COM/ABPANPHOTO
YOUTUBE.COM/ABPANPHOTO
TWITTER.COM/ABPANPHOTO

QUICK REFERENCE

LINCOLN MEMORIAL *5-18*

LINCOLN MEMORIAL REFLECTING POOL *19-26*

VIETNAM VETERANS MEMORIAL *30-36*

NATIONAL WORLD WAR II MEMORIAL *37-43*

DISTRICT OF COLUMBIA WAR MEMORIAL *44-48*

WASHINGTON MONUMENT *51-62*

JEFFERSON MEMORIAL *66-76*

FLORAL LIBRARY *77-81*

MARTIN LUTHER KING JR MEMORIAL *82-88*

CHERRY BLOSSOMS *89-99*

KUTZ BRIDGE *101-106*

CONSTITUTION GARDENS *109-112*

ENID A HAUPT GARDENS *113-118*

WHITE HOUSE *120-123*

US CAPITOL BUILDING *124-138*

LIBRARY OF CONGRESS *139-144*

JAMES MADISON MEMORIAL *145-146*

UNION STATION *149-154*

ARLINGTON MEMORIAL BRIDGE *155-161*

UNITED STATES MARINE CORPS WAR MEMORIAL *162-166*

NETHERLANDS CARILLON *167-171*

UNITED STATES AIR FORCE MEMORIAL *172-180*

UNITED STATES NATIONAL ARBORETUM *181-187*

ROCK CREEK PARK *188-192*

GREAT FALLS NATIONAL PARK *193-197*

SCOTT'S RUN NATURE PRESERVE *198-200*